SEE ME. *NOW*

SEE ME. *NOW*

Authors

Rafiq Williams
Dr. Joyce Vottima Jeuell
Anne Fahy Morris

Editor

Dr. Sasha Eloi Evans

Copyright © 2025
SEE ME. NOW, LLC

All rights reserved.
ISBN: 979-8-9906940-6-4
Hardback ISBN: 979-8-9906940-7-1

All rights reserved. No portion of this book may be produced mechanically, electronically, or by any other means, including photocopying without written permission of the authors.

Authors' Notes

It was a summer graduate class, and students were introducing themselves. I had asked them to talk about their current positions and to share something fun or unusual about their life. When it was Rafiq Williams' turn, he talked about his job, title, then about his life as a teenager when he was driving a champagne-colored Lexus at age 16. If my thoughts had wandered before, I was paying rapt attention now. He continued to share about his life and how his journey had brought him to my graduate class. When he was finished, I told him if he ever wanted to tell his story, I would help write it. – *J. V. J*

I struggled to find a word that could capture all of Rafiq Williams. A broad stroke word like "strong," is true, but it fails to capture the interesting layers, the nooks and the crannies that equally contribute to Williams' unique essence. Williams discovered the Bible, and in the years since, he has tried to live a Christian life. Having witnessed his faith in good times and bad over several years, having followed him in his role of principal as research for this book, having met weekly for almost three years, a word finally came to me. He is a shepherd. He is one to trust to guide you to where the grazing is good. Yet, at the same time,

Williams is as humble as a lamb and as strong as an ox.

– *A. F. M*

To contact the authors email us at:
seemenow1098@gmail.com

Dedication

From Rafiq Williams

- To **my Lord and Savior, Jesus Christ**—the author of my story, the anchor of my soul, and the redeemer of my past. Without You, none of this would exist. All honor, all glory, all praise belongs to You.
- To my **grandmother, Lula Williams, whom we affectionately call "Grem,"** thank you for introducing me to Christ and planting the seed of faith that continues to grow in me daily.
- To my **mother, Yolanda Williams**, and my **father, Michael Williams**, your love, sacrifices, and stressful situations that we found ourselves in laid the foundation for the man I've become.
- To my **wife, Sharon Hamilton**—you are my light, my peace, and the one who believes in me without hesitation. Your love gave me the courage to finish what I once only dreamed of starting.

To my children:

- **Lionell** *(Arti)* – You made me a father before I knew how to be one. You matured me and gave me purpose.

- **Rafiq Jr.** *(Rowdy)* – My soldier. You embody the best parts of me from a time when I couldn't live them out.
- **Shanyia** *(Peaches)* – The first girl I ever truly loved and wasn't afraid to show it to. The one who contributed to the first grays in my beard, and gave me even more joy at the same time.
- **Darius** *(Dar)* – You stood beside me when I fully submitted my life to Christ. Your encouragement kept me going when I desperately wanted to give up.
- **Cheyanne** *(Cheytown)* – You remind me of the fighter in me—focused, fearless, and relentless.
- **Emmi** *(EM&M)* – Your natural gift of doing hair and creativity echoes a part of my journey, which included self-teaching and growth.
- **Savanna** *(Turkey Meatloaf)* – Your hugs and heart for Jesus at such a young age humble and inspire me. You keep me grounded in my walk with God.

To my brothers:
- **Ercel Ballenger** *(Erc)* – My eldest brother. You've always had my back, always encouraged me, and never let me forget my worth.
- **Michael Williams Jr.** *(Meat)* – You and I walked through some of the darkest chapters in this story, especially one in particular. To know what that is,

you'll have to read it. But thank you for surviving it with me.

This book is a tribute to the lives, love, and faith that shaped me. This is for all of you.

From Dr. Joyce Vottima Jeuell

- They say it takes a village to raise a child, which I believe. But I also know it took a village to support and guide me as I faced the unexpected and untimely death of my beloved husband, **Al**. The **Sisters of St. Joseph at Chestnut Hill College**, were my village—my pillars of strength, prayer, and support. I am eternally grateful for their presence in my life.
- **To Chestnut Hill College**, where I met a very bright, kind, and articulate graduate student named **Rafiq Williams**. His honesty and candor touched my heart and sparked a desire to help him tell his story—one that the world truly needs to hear.
- To my sons, **Peter and Alex Hellberg**—thank you for always giving me purpose, love, and a bit of anxiety. And to the strong women you brought into our family, **Karin and Gina**—thank you for saving me (often!) from your husbands' antics.
- I thought my life was truly blessed—then came my grandchildren: **Drew, Ava, and Wren Hellberg**. What a joy it is to be loved by you. You keep me young and on my tippy toes.

- Finally, to **Dale Hollenbach**—a friend from high school who once gave me rides home in 11th grade, and 50 years later, helped mend a broken heart. You've been a part of my healing journey in ways words can't fully capture.

To all of you, thank you. You are truly the wind beneath my wings.

From Anne Fahy Morris

- To the Father, the Son, and the Holy Spirit. We asked You to join us in this journey. This work would not be here without You.
- To the professors at the Graduate School of Education at the University of Pennsylvania for inspiring their students to make the world a better place.
- To **Dr. Joyce Jeuell,** who invited me into this project. Your leadership, vision, and heart brought us all together.
- And to my favorite people—**Wilson, Natalie, Caroline, & Luke Morris, and Becca Strickler,** your love and laughter are everything to me.

Thank you to the many who have walked this journey with me.

Preface

This is the true story of Rafiq Williams, a journey that spans 48 years. Today, Williams is a beloved Dean of Students at a large public high school in Delaware—but the path that brought him here was anything but easy. This work stands as living proof that it is possible to rise above the hardest circumstances and help others do the same. It is for the person who needs to believe, *"If he did it, I can do it."* Williams does not sugarcoat his mistakes or the traumas he endured. His experiences—both the victories and the hardships—built an iron-clad resilience and a belief in himself when no one else believed.

This work is honest, sometimes raw, and entirely authentic—hence the title, *See Me. Now.* Certain expressions, while unacceptable in today's language, are included for the sake of accuracy and are attributed directly to the speaker. For all who read these words, may you see something of yourself in these pages and find hope, strength, and the reminder that no matter where you begin, your story is still yours to write.

Table Of Contents

Chapter I The Wolf 2

Chapter II On The Run 20

Chapter III The Corner 38

Chapter IV Locked Up 49

Chapter V Doin' Your Bid 65

Chapter VI The Trial 94

Chapter VII The Cartel 107

Chapter VIII Disobedience 123

Chapter IX Real Love 132

Chapter X Rebirth 149

He leads confidently toward the good because he has seen enough bad. No predicament is too daunting for the strong will, resilience, and hope he inspires. Walk beside him in this story and see where it leads you...

You have heard that when life gives you lemons, make lemonade. The problem is that having all the ingredients doesn't ensure you can make lemonade when you have never been taught how to make lemonade. This was my life until I learned how.

Rafiq Williams

Chapter I The Wolf

She was angry. Very angry with me. It wasn't just the rage flashing in her eyes but the butcher knife she was wielding in her hand. Even as a 13-year-old, seeing my mom like that, I knew my options were limited—run or die. As she brought the knife forward, I pushed her to avoid being stabbed and started running for my life. I could hear my mom screaming, *"You bet not come back; you gon' put ya' hands on me? I brought you into this world, and now I will take you out of it!"* I just kept running.

I wasn't sure where to go, but I knew I had to keep running. Going home wasn't an option. I ran for what seemed like an hour, and when I finally stopped, I was faced with the reality and severity of what just happened. My mind was all over the place, where would I go, would anyone let me stay with them, how would I survive on my own in this world? But I was sure of one thing: If I was going to survive, I would need to be a wolf to pull it off.

We studied various animals in school, and I became intrigued with wolves. A wolf is viewed by many as a dangerous animal and is avoided at every cost. Wolves travel in packs and generally have a pack leader.

When threatened, a wolf is very dangerous and will attack until the threat is neutralized, usually that means death. As a 13-year-old living on the street, having a group of friends, my pack was vital, and I needed to let everyone know that when threatened, or disrespected, I would turn into a savage beast that is ready to kill should the need arise.

Living like a wolf made logical sense to me at that time. I couldn't afford for anyone to find out that secretly I was a scared little boy, and living life as a wolf provided the camouflage needed until I grew in stature and reputation.

The roots of my homelessness began after visiting my dad in prison. Before my dad served time in a federal prison, he was housed at the Philadelphia Industrial Correctional Center (P.I.C.C). But, on that fateful day in 1991, my mom, my brother Mike, my cousin Jim, and I visited my dad to celebrate him earning his GED.

Though it was supposed to be a joyful celebration, my dad pulled me aside and began to get on me for not paying the car notes and bills for my mom. He had depended on me to do these things after entering the family business. My pop continued to berate me telling me that I was pissing him off. Finally,
when I couldn't take him getting on me any longer, I told him, *"The reason I am not giving her any money is because I saw her kiss another man!"*

Once he realized what I just said, my dad yelled, *"Back the fuck up, what did you just say?"* as if he needed to make sure he heard me correctly. I repeated what I saw one morning between my mom and another man after she had come home from a night of partying. My pop called my mom over to where we were sitting and confronted her with this information. I was hurt because my mom didn't realize that I saw what she did with this man.

I saw the hurt and anger in my dad's face, and, at that moment, I wished I could disappear. I always wanted to please him, and now I just delivered some news that knocked the life out of him. I felt sad but didn't show it. But unfortunately, there was no escaping the repercussion of that moment. My mom shouted, *"You a damn liar."* But I was adamant and stood my ground because I knew what I saw. I began describing the man's green car parked in front of our house to my mom and dad and how the man had opened the screen door, because the front door was open, and leaned in to kiss her. I saw the anger in my mom's face, but I didn't care because she had betrayed my dad.

Shocked by this turn of events, my dad's reaction was swift and painful, telling me that even though he was alive in prison, we should consider him dead now. My mom was hot with me for ratting her out.

The car ride home from PICC with my mom, Mike, and Jim was eerily silent. You could hear the noise from the tires colliding with the street as we drove home. The ride home seemed like it took forever, and the silence was killing me. Many thoughts began to run through my mind. Thoughts like, is she about to smack me at any moment, is she about to curse me out. I hoped that she would say something, but she said nothing.

I'm her child, she wouldn't hurt me too bad would she, is another thought that repeatedly went through my mind. I knew from previous observations that my mom wasn't dangerous when she was loud. But when she was silent, I never knew what to expect. I knew the consequences of this would be explosive, and man was I right. But I had no idea of the magnitude of how my life was about to change, and change it did, immediately.

Battle lines were drawn and for me, there would be no more celebratory days, only the harsh realities of a life of homelessness and hopelessness initially. Before my dad was incarcerated, my older brother, Michael, who was named after our father, and I, grew up in a brick-row home on Douglas Street in the Strawberry Mansion section of North Philadelphia.

For us, life was often a challenge as our mom was an addict and eventually was not able to keep providing a strong, nurturing, and supportive environment. She was rarely home day or night. If she was home, she spent most of her time high or sleeping. But the one thing she did teach us when she was home was proper hygiene. That way, there would be no reason for anybody from the school to assume anything was messed up at home.

My mom may have been an addict, but she kept a clean house. And, as part of our culture in the hood, what happened in our house stayed in our house. My mom always told us, *"Y'all know what happens in my house stays in my house, so don't even think about saying nothing to nobody 'bout what's going on up in here!"*

As a child, I was an observer, always watching what was happening around me in the streets, at my cousins' houses, and school. I wanted to know everything. Who to stay away from, how to act around certain people, when to speak, when not to speak, and most importantly, how to spot something that ain't right, because that typically meant danger was near.

We got up and got ready for school by ourselves most days. We were bused to Greenberg Elementary School in the Northeast section of Philadelphia. Ironically, our often-absent mom made a case with the school district personnel that her boys should be bussed to Greenburg, which was about 15 miles from our home on Douglas Street because it would provide her boys with a better education.

My mom was a pro at manipulating the system. She would tell us on many occasions, *"People can take a lot of things from you, but they can't take away your education. So, when you go to school, you pay attention."* I was one of less than 10 black kids at that school which was kindergarten to sixth grade.

I was good academically, but my behavior was another story. I completed all of my homework assignments, I was relatively attentive and focused in class, and initially, I stayed out of trouble at school. I loved to learn as a child, I had aspirations of being a lawyer one day. While my home life may have been lonely and chaotic, at least when I was at school, there was something consistent and safe in my life. I took my mom's words to heart about the importance of an education.

One continuing bright spot in my life was my grandmother Lula Mae Williams, whom we affectionately called Grem, lived directly across the street from us. My Grem was a hardworking, devout Christian woman whom I looked at as a pillar of strength. She was a seamstress in a factory in Philadelphia doing piecework, and she also sewed for others from her home.

I would go to her house on the weekends, which I loved. Many of my cousins would be there too. She was strict and made sure we followed her rules which were: no slang talk, no loud talking, no running around the house, always saying that her house *"ain't no playground,"* and we better not interrupt when adults are talking. We all followed her rules.

I especially remember the delicious breakfasts and Sunday dinners my Grem would make. Her breakfasts were often pork bacon, scrambled eggs with cheese, grits with cheese, and toast. My dad, who was a Muslim at the time, usually complained to Grem about serving us pork and playing gospel music. But Grem just smiled and continued to serve us whatever she made, saying, *"If they eat at my house, they will eat what I make, and in this house, we eat pork."*

All of my Grem's grandchildren came to her house for Sunday dinners, as did the neighbors who lived on the block. Often there would be 15 or more for Grem's collard greens and baked macaroni and cheese. And music, there was always gospel music playing. My Grem affectionately called me "Ra" or "Fiqqi." I was one of just a few of the 11 grandchildren to whom she gave a nickname, yet I feel that she treated all of us the same.

Even with a loving grandmother, my life was rather bleak, as my brother, and I continued to self-care. We were fortunate to have a roof over our heads, clothing to wear, and a refrigerator that generally held the essentials—eggs, milk, bread, and butter. Before we could barely reach above the stove, my brother and I would often make scrambled egg sandwiches or boil Oodles of Noodles, chicken flavor, adding hot sauce and Old Bay seasoning, believe it or not, it was good that way. Occasionally we would have biscuits with syrup. We would pretend that they were pancakes.

I remember times when there wasn't any food, and my brother, my mom, and I would steal food from the supermarket. My mom would say, *"You don't steal just to steal; you only steal to survive."* So, we stole biscuits, eggs, and crab meat. I never really understood why we stole crabmeat; it never filled us up anyway. I remember thinking to myself, like why do we have to steal food since my dad was a member of the Junior Black Mafia and a notorious drug dealer who made plenty of money. He was a high-ranking member of the organization.

I remember meeting AJ (Aaron Jones, the Leader) many times as a kid, but at the time I didn't know what he did for a living. My dad sold a lot of drugs for the "M" (nickname for the J.B.M). Being recognized as the child of a J.B.M. member brought a level of safety and respect that was comforting. As a high-ranking member, he had his own set of enforcers that my brother and I were very close to. The JBM was an African American organized crime syndicate in Philadelphia that operated from 1985 to 1992 and was involved in numerous criminal activities, including drug trafficking and murder.

As a seven-year-old, life was pretty stressful, I was never sure about having enough food or if our clothes would be clean. When she found the time, my mom washed our clothes across the street at Grem's house. My mom was a party girl, who was frequently absent for hours, and sometimes days at a time. But she did arrange to have an older cousin of ours, from my pop's side of the family, Lil' Tony, who was about 17 stop over and watch my brother and me, particularly on weekends and occasionally after school.

I knew that everyone loved Lil' Tony. Even though Lil' Tony wasn't "hard" like most of the other boys, he was loved in my family, especially by my mom. But for Mike and me, it was as if our mom had let the devil into our house. Lil' Tony began sexually abusing us within the first few weeks of coming over to watch us when my mom went out. I was shocked to find out as I got older that this traumatizing event is somewhat common in families throughout the country, crossing racial lines and socioeconomic statuses. We were always taught to avoid strangers and the ploys they may use to lure children to them, but no one ever taught us how to avoid predatory family members.

The abuse began as wrestling games which progressed further for years. I tried to reconcile in my mind how everyone could love Lil' Tony, even Grem, while he was physically hurting my brother and me. I was afraid to tell anyone about the abuse and Mike, and

I swore each other to secrecy about what Lil' Tony was doing to us. I feared that even if I did tell my mom, she would choose Lil' Tony over me, I wouldn't be believed, and I would be left feeling abandoned. I was very confused and wondered, *"Is this, okay?" Is it not okay?"* I was angry and I felt helpless because of Lil' Tony's size and the age difference. The anger within me grew.

As a seven-year-old, I knew I hated Lil' Tony, but I felt I had to mask my feelings because everyone else loved him. My hatred for him was deep, so deep that I didn't attend Lil' Tony's funeral when he died in 1994 years after he had contracted HIV which progressed to AIDS. I had even envisioned shooting Lil' Tony, but I knew that Grem would be hurt, and wouldn't be able to handle it. It was because of my love and respect for Grem, that I never acted on my feelings. Here I am yet once again having to put my feelings aside to prevent hurting another. But I was certain of one thing---no one else would ever be able to take advantage of me, physically or otherwise, without severe consequences.

Even though I had to take care of and stand up for myself from a very young age, family members saw me as sensitive and kind. My pop, however, saw me differently, often referring to me as such a "faggot" and a momma's boy for crying all the time. Consequently, my pop's negative rants made me feel like I was soft, and I didn't want to be identified with anything resembling Lil' Tony. Hearing this constant refrain from my dad, I worked at being something different than what he saw me as, I wanted to show him that I wasn't like that. I was tougher than he thought!

On the heels of the abuse by my cousin, and still a young child, I learned a skill that would eventually haunt me when I was older, I learned how to shut down my emotions. I learned that I had to become something other than sensitive and kind. I had to become something and someone else altogether. I had to show my pop I wasn't soft and ain't nothing weak about me, I ain't a momma's boy, and I ain't no "faggot" as dad used to call me.

Thinking about all of this, I felt that being seen as hard would be the best approach, and I began to create a new self. I also began getting into trouble at school and in the hood. I got into fistfights with neighborhood boys, cursed a lot, and would walk away from my block even though I was told not to. I also broke curfew frequently, for which I received many whuppings from my dad with a belt or extension cord. The making of the wolf in me began to take shape, and it felt good.

For the new, hard version of me, Greenberg Elementary became an escape from my everyday life. I got to play with other kids my age and could avoid the reality of needing to be this hard guy all of the time, which was slowly becoming a conflict for me internally. Trying to ignore the conflict, I continued my quest to grow up being hard and added sex as part of my new persona. My brother and I started watching soft porn movies after midnight on television. We would watch this on HBO, typically in the wee hours of the morning. This was when HBO could only be viewed on the little brown box with a silver switch on it.

When I was 11, I started having sex with a 10-year-old neighborhood girl. Not long after we began experimenting, the little girl got knocked up. When my pop found out, initially, he did not seem concerned, knowing he could pay my way out of it. But then, in front of me, he would appear angry, and he told me that I was too young to have a kid since I was still only a young kid myself. Because my dad was an active member of the J.B.M., the pregnant girl's parents didn't want that smoke[1] from my family. There was an inherent fear and respect from others in the community for the J.B.M. due to their ruthless, get down or lay down, mantra. The pregnant girl's parents simply asked for $1500 to take care of things.

My pop paid the family and sternly told me: he was only going to take care of one such problem. I would be on my own if anything like this happened again. Feeling confused, frustrated, angry, very alone, and scared at the

---

[1] Smoke—problems leading to violence

thought of having a baby as an 11-year-old, I went upstairs to my room to be alone.

Later that evening, my parents had some friends over and were smoking weed and doing other drugs, and I could hear my pop boasting about his boy getting that little girl knocked up, saying, that's my boy! He laughed about it and applauded that his son was having sex and was not gay. Even though I was only 11, my pop never questioned me about how I learned about sex. I was further confused by my pop's reaction to me because it didn't match how he was reacting to my mom and their friends that night. My mom quietly disagreed with the boasting from my dad, and at some point, I heard her say, *"Aye, Mike, cut it out. Don't be saying that. That's my baby you talking 'bout!"* I ultimately felt that my parents were proud of what had happened with the neighborhood girl. Perhaps this hard persona was working after all.

Despite the challenges and adverse childhood experiences, I was still hoping to be a lawyer one day. That is until my 6th-grade teacher told me I should focus on custodial careers, saying I would be more suited to be a janitor. School seemed like it should be important; my mom certainly thought so as I could frequently hear her words, *"Be sure to pay attention."* She also said that if you want to hide something from a Black person, put it in a book.

Learning and remembering information came easily to me, and I earned good grades, I participated in class, and I completed my homework assignments. I had a hunger to learn. I liked school because I could lose myself there and did not have to think about my family life, my home situation, and my dad's territory.

My brother Mike began teasing me because he thought that I sounded and acted White. Even my cousins made fun of me because I earned good grades. They said, *"You're a nerd, you ain't that smart, and you just trying to be White."* I was conflicted about how I should act, what I should be doing, and who I should be. To keep developing my wolf persona, I decided it would be best to be hard, even in school.

As a result of my new behaviors, I started getting suspended. But I did not bully anyone at school. I hated bullies! I went out of my way to help those kids who were bullied by others. One day I observed another student forcibly taking a Transformer toy from a classmate. I snatched the Transformer back and returned it to the boy it belonged to, as he was about to cry. I would intervene whenever I saw bigger kids harassing smaller, younger ones telling them, *"Don't pick with him, pick with me if you think you're that tough."*

I didn't mind fighting at this point, it helped to build my new persona. There was a level of aggression building in me that I couldn't understand or articulate to anyone who would ask me why I was so angry.

When I wasn't acting hard, I was trying to be the class clown. I also became increasingly disrespectful to my teachers. If a teacher asked me to sit down, I would say, you can't tell me what to do; you ain't my mom. I felt my code-switching was working. However, my behavior and mocking of my teachers frequently landed me in the principal's office.

Mr. Romanelli, the principal, was a large man with a limited string of black hair wrapped around his bald head, thick black glasses, and a heavy black mustache. Once I was with Mr. Romanelli, I would go into full code switch, telling him, *"I was trying to pay attention, Mr. Romanelli. Why would I lie to you?"* I became a frequent flier to Mr. Romanelli's office, and he would tell me that I was smart, and ask me why couldn't I stay out of trouble? And I would respond with, I think the teachers just don't like me, Mr. Romanelli. When in actuality, many of the mostly White teachers were afraid of me.

I could tell when people were scared, you could see it in their actions; they were afraid to come too close to you. Like dogs, you can sense someone else's fear, you can smell it a mile away. I learned this skill of sensing fear from the hood. I felt no connection or attachment to anyone at the school, yet people wanted to hang around with me. I was slowly building my street cred.

Regardless of my multiple excuses, the principal had to call home about my behavior. When Mr. Romanelli eventually reached my mom, she bought whatever I had said. But my pop would say, *"Oh Hell no! You think you slick, but you ain't slicker than me,"*
my pop yelled. *"You are dumb as hell if you think I am believing you."* As a result, I often got a whupping at home for my school antics.

It was important to me that my pop saw me as tough, even tougher than he was. As I grew into a teenage boy and young man he regretted what he had turned me into. He never said it, but I could tell by the way he would look at me sometimes due to things he was hearing on the streets and from family members. As my bravado at school began to grow, people were intrigued and wanted to hang around with the bad boy.

By the time I was in 8th grade at Baldi Middle School, I was both respected and feared. I began wearing gold chains to school, carrying large sums of money and handguns. I even lied to the school administration saying that I was receiving $500 a week from my pop for my allowance whenever they would ask me questions.

This angered my pop because he believed my words and actions would bring heat to his illegal activities with the

J.B.M. He knew that to be able to give me $500 a week totals $24,000 a year, and he would have to have a really good job to do so. In his mind, this would bring questions that he didn't have the answers to, and once any law enforcement agency took a hard look, they would eventually find what he had been trying to keep hidden for so long, his illegal drug activities. He never really knew the extent of what I was bringing to school because I would never wear those things in his presence.

    I began experimenting with selling drugs in West Philadelphia with my homies Mal (Jamal) and Riq (Tariq). It was the suspicion, or should I say racial profiling, that led to speculation of me carrying guns that prompted frequent checks of my locker at school. I must admit their suspicion was correct. So, I decided to hide the weapons outside the school by the track.

    I already knew how to use a gun, having found one under my dad's pillow one day when I was nine years old. I examined the gun and pointed it toward the couch and pulled the trigger. I heard the loud bang and saw smoke come out of the hole in the couch. My ears were ringing and I realized the gun was real. I figured since the couch was a brown color, no one would be able to see the hole in the cushion, and no one ever did. Then I put the gun back under my dad's pillow.

Changing locations means nothing without a change in one's mentality.

Rafiq Williams

Chapter II On the Run

There were plenty of times when I wished my parents were dead. Whenever my brother and I got into trouble, Mike was never punished as much as I was. I was often subjected to ridicule from my dad and my brother. But I was honing my skills of becoming a wolf, intensely strong, fierce even, protecting my family and shoring up my abilities to be the man I thought my pop wanted me to be. I would need to be strong, very strong as my mom was spiraling downward from the drug abuse.

Because of the continuous lack of supervision at home, sometimes for five consecutive days, my brother and I would often be on the streets from dawn to late at night. One of our neighbors, Veronica Underwood, whom we affectionately called Aunt Veronica, continually yelled at us, *"Get back around the corner and go in the house."* She knew we could be trouble or get into it being out that late at night on the streets. Many times, she would walk Mike and me home and wait until we went into the house before she left. As hard as I was becoming, nothing quite prepared me for my mom's suicide attempt.

One afternoon when my mom was home, she sent me to my maternal grandmother Elaine's house a few blocks away. I was nine years old at the time and I loved having my mom at home. So I was confused and disappointed when she sent me away. I just wanted to be home with my mom. I adored my mom and always obeyed what she said, so very reluctantly I left.

Unbeknownst to me, Lil' Tony had decided to go visit my mom that same afternoon. Lil' Tony knocked on the door several times but got no answer. So, Lil' Tony opened the mail slot in the front door to call out to her, which people frequently did when no one answered. As soon as he pushed the brass mail slot open, the gas smell rushed out. Lil' Tony kicked the door in and found my mom unconscious on the couch.

My mom had ingested a slew of pills, leaving an empty bottle, and to ensure that her life would be over, she had turned on the gas. Lil' Tony kept calling my mom's name and shaking her, but he could not wake her. That's when Lil' Tony called 911 and rushed across the street to get Grem. My mom was rushed by ambulance to Women's Medical Hospital, also known as MCP, for emergency care.

Later that afternoon, my grandmom Elaine received a phone call from my dad, and she began crying. After she hung up the phone, she told me that my mom had tried to kill herself, but the doctors were able to save her. I just started crying. I was scared, confused, and angry. I couldn't understand why my mom would do this, I had so many questions and I wondered if her suicide attempt was my fault. Had I done something to cause this?

I didn't allow myself to cry for too long. Hearing my dad calling me a "faggot" in my mind instantly dried up the tears. I just went out on my grand mom Elaine's porch, gathered my thoughts, and returned to the house as if nothing had happened.

After a week in the hospital, my mom was transferred to Friends Hospital, where she stayed for 60 days. My brother and I were sent to live with different grandparents. I stayed with my grandmom Elaine and Mike went to stay with Grem. My confusion became even more intense and I was never given a chance to visit my mom while she was in the hospital. Neither did my brother; however, my dad went to see her about two or three times.

Living with grandmom Elaine was very different for me. There was much more structure and rules in place, and she didn't play. She would cuss me out from A to Z if I got on her nerves or did something she didn't like. Once I got in trouble when I went in the refrigerator without asking for permission, and another time, I got smacked for chewing with my mouth open, often referred to as smacking in the hood, at the dinner table.

Still, I knew she loved me, I could just feel it. Grandmom Elaine would always hug me and tell me how much she loved me. She would often say how much I resembled my mom, her daughter. Whenever my dad wouldn't call to check on me or come by to see me, even after promising he would, my grandmom would tell me not to worry about it. She made me feel loved when at that time, I felt very unloved and alone, resulting from the constant disappointments from my pop. When my mom finally returned home, she told me that she just felt like giving up. Life was just getting too hard.

My mom, Yolanda, who was also known as Plunky, had a challenging life growing up in North Philadelphia. Her family was close and money was tight. She was raised by her mom Elaine and her stepfather, Ray Ballenger. She was the second youngest of five children. Two of her siblings, Renee and Michael, had been given up for adoption as babies, and another sister, Lulu, had been killed while serving in the military.
Her brother Tommy was a heroin addict who died when he was in his 30s.

While she had been one of five children, she grew up as an only child. Her mom, Elaine, my grandmom, had expectations of her daughter, and following rules was number one. Even though my mom was a capable student academically, she was often in trouble for fighting and skipping school. When she was around 11 or 12, my grandmom sent my mom to boarding school, which my mom hated.

During the few months she was at the boarding school, my grandmom would receive weekly phone calls from the school administrators that Plunky had run away from the school grounds. Finally, after several weeks she was expelled from the school and sent home. But my mom never really went back to her home, instead, she moved from house to house living with her friends and their families.

Although she had been in love with my dad, Mike Sr., since she was in grade school, at 14, she became pregnant by Mustang, a young man who also lived in their neighborhood. My grandmom was very angry that my mom got herself pregnant—another rule had been broken. My mom was 15 when her son, whom she named Ercel, was born. Erc, as me and my brother Mike call him, was raised by my grandmom, Elaine, from birth. It would be years before I even knew that Erc was my half-brother, not my uncle.

When my mom was 16, my parents, who had grown up on the same block, got back together again. They were married in a small ceremony at Grem's house. When my mom was 17 and my dad was 18, she gave birth to my brother, Mike. As a new wife and mother, she did not finish high school and never really held a job outside the house. She liked to socialize and party with friends, which she did often, and was generally known as a party girl. The following year, when she was 18, I was born. Motherhood did not interfere with my mom's party lifestyle. It seemed to further enhance her social standing and her recreational drug use which continued for years.

So much of life converged on my mom that summer day when she sent me to my grandmom Elaine's house—most of which I knew nothing about. Maybe her suicide attempt was a reflection of the choices she had made and the many struggles and sorrows she endured for so many years. All I knew was that my beloved mom had almost died and none of the adults in my life would tell me anything.

As a nine-year-old, I felt completely helpless. Being without my mom was extremely sad and difficult and I had difficulty sleeping and maintaining focus. I didn't even have my brother Mike to talk with since my dad had sent him to Grem's house that day, and Erc and I weren't that close at this time.

That sadness and fear eventually turned into anger because I could not comprehend why the mom, whom I loved and adored would have wanted to leave me without a mother. But I also knew my dad expected me to be tough and show no emotion or fear about what had happened to my mom. But fear was a constant feeling for me, fear that I could lose my mom for good.

Now that my mom was finally home, things at home seemed weird. My pop had an answer to this upheaval; he packed up the family and moved us from Douglas Street to the Luxury Apartments on Roosevelt Boulevard in the Northeast section of Philadelphia.

My pop was a man who took care of things, his family, his friends, and his associates. So, moving his family to a luxury apartment was his way of taking care of my mom and moving past her suicide attempt, a topic that was never discussed in the family.

Initially, my pop was attentive to my mom after she returned home. While I felt my parents loved each other, there was no outward display of that love, at least not in front of my brother and me. A relatively tall man at 5"11", my pop had a muscular build and commanded attention. He did not tolerate weaknesses or show any kind of emotion. Any display of affection was a sign of weakness.

Growing up on the same block as my mom in North Philadelphia, my dad was the middle child, with three brothers and one sister. He wasn't academically focused and dropped out of Murrell Dobbins Vocational High School in North Philadelphia in 10th grade. He didn't enjoy studying, but his basketball skills were well-known in the community. Unfortunately, by not pursuing his education, any hopes of playing in high school and beyond were quickly diminished.

After they were married, my dad focused on learning carpentry skills and remodeling houses in the area to support my mom, brother, and me. But my pop quickly turned in his hammer for the fast life of dealing marijuana in the neighborhood slowly building his clientele.

During that time, a close friend of my dad, named Black Kev, who was like an uncle to my brother and me, introduced my dad to the J.B.M. This allowed him to take his drug dealing to new heights. Since my dad was earning substantially more money as a drug dealer with the J.B.M. the move to the luxury apartments was relatively seamless.

Initially, the new apartment, with two bedrooms on the first floor and plenty of large windows, was an excellent place to live. What I loved most about the new apartment was the swimming pool, which was available for all tenants. I would swim every day during the spring and summer months once the pool opened. This was much different than the neighborhood public pools we would use. This pool was clean, with plenty of lounge chairs around the pool, and didn't have a lifeguard on duty. Whenever family visited us the first thing they usually asked about was the pool. It was located in a courtyard around other apartments. Unfortunately, my brother and I were ultimately banned from using the pool for skinny dipping. If I am one hundred percent honest, I was mostly the one skinny dipping. With the accessibility we had to the pool, I felt like it was ours.

Our new apartment was also within walking distance of the Northeast Mall on Cottman Avenue and Roosevelt Boulevard. Another perk was the central air, this was a huge improvement from our last house, which used window units for air conditioning. I also remember a couple of lavish

Christmases at the apartment that were special because my brother and I had dozens of gifts from Toys R Us and Kiddie City. The packages were colorfully wrapped beneath a large, real Christmas tree that we had spent the afternoon decorating each Christmas we spent here.

We even had an arcade game in our apartment, it was a Ms. Pacman and Donkey Kong Jr. combo game and all the old neighborhood kids and our cousins wanted to come to our spot. But my feelings of joy and excitement about our new home were quickly shattered once I realized that my brother and I would be left alone most of the time again, fending for ourselves.

Living in the luxury apartments was also the first time I experienced blatant racism. There was an incident where I was walking across Roosevelt Boulevard coming from McDonald's when a passenger in a passing car spat in my face and called me a nigger.

Another time my brothers and I were coming home from Orleans 8, a movie theater in the area, and we were approached by two White plainclothes detectives and searched. They told us that someone had just been robbed at gunpoint, and we fit the description of the alleged robbers. We were thrown into the back of an unmarked police car and driven to where the victim was to see if he could identify us as the robbers; however, the elderly White man told the police none of us was the guy who robbed him. You talk about being scared, we were all scared at that moment because we were certain that the man would identify us as the robber, even though we knew we hadn't robbed anyone. We had just come from the movies, still had the movie stubs on us, and showed them to the officers, but we were still hauled off to the scene of a robbery, not to mention the victim being an elderly white man.

Coming from the hood we had either seen or heard how these events usually end. Thankfully, and thankful we were, this didn't end the way we had either seen before or heard of.

When we returned home to our apartment and told my mom what had just taken place, she got angry, instantly she called 911, and asked to speak with a lieutenant or captain. A white captain and a uniformed officer, who was also white, showed up from the second district police department. My mom began telling the captain what just happened to us and how it was illegal to question juveniles without a guardian and especially, to take them to the scene of a crime. She was very animated while saying this.

The captain told my mom that she better calm down before he locked her up. Not backing down, she said, *"Don't tell me what to do or how to talk in my house. Your officer violated my children's rights and I want to know what you are going to do about it!"* The captain continued to justify his officer's actions and told my mom that if she didn't like it, she should move. My mom kicked the officers out of our house at that comment using a few choice words.

In that moment the way she dealt with those cops she was my hero. She made us feel that she had our backs, but I couldn't escape thinking, where was this type of support when me and my brother were getting sexually abused by our cousin? I quickly suppressed that thought and basked in the moment.

The luxury apartment was also where I blocked out all negative things, especially the physical abuse suffered at the hands of my cousin, Lil' Tony. It was as if that part of my life had just been in my imagination.

During the initial weeks of my mom's return from the hospital and living in the luxury apartment, she was loving, patient, nurturing, and above all, present. But slowly, as she began to use drugs again, the loving,
attentive mother began to disappear. I fantasized about having a different family, like the one on the Cosby Show that I liked watching on television. A mom who was home with the kids, who helped with their homework, who took them places, who cooked meals so they could eat together.

When I thought about my life, it just seemed, well, chaotic. And over time, I learned to navigate the ongoing chaos rather easily. Several years passed and one day, everything in my life was about to explode. If I thought my life was tumultuous before, it was time for me to lace up my boots and flaunt the wolf-like exterior.

One fall afternoon, my mom picked me up from school early and brought me home. Mike, who was a distinguished high school athlete at George Washington High School, had football practice after school, and interrupting that was not an option. When we arrived home, my pop was there with my Uncle Ab (short for Abdul) and one of his enforcers named Prince.

The FBI had executed predawn raids on my pop's clubhouse and Grem's house, and he told me, *"Now, they are coming for me, but I ain't 'bout to let them catch me slippin'."*

My mom started crying uncontrollably, but my pop was dismissive of her crying restating the urgency of his need to bounce[2] and taking one of his sons with him. He told me that I would be the one going with him.

The plan was to head straight down I-95 to Decatur, Georgia, to hide out at a relative's house, my Uncle Butch. I was about 12 at the time, and I noticed large black trash bags in the car's trunk filled with clothes and guns. My dad was paranoid and anxious to get on the road. Still crying and knowing there were no other options, my mom hugged

---

[2] Bounce—leave

me tightly, for what seemed like an eternity, and said goodbye.

I had no idea how long I would be away from my mom and brother, but I felt as though this would be the last time that I might see her. My parents switched cars to make it more difficult for the FBI to track us while my dad was trying to avoid being caught. We were ready to leave, but for some reason, my pop also wanted to take my mom's dog, a miniature black poodle named Dominque.

We were headed down I-95 and stopped briefly in Virginia for gas. Eventually, I fell asleep at a rest stop. I was in the backseat, my pop in the front seat, and Uncle Ab and Prince were sitting in the grass just outside of the car. When we reached North Carolina, a friend of my dad's, Lev, met us there. He had tickets for us to attend the North Carolina A&T homecoming game. It was an interesting distraction from the chaotic way we left Philly and had raced down I-95 for hours. It was also confusing to think that my pop was trying to evade capture by the FBI yet here we were sitting at a college football game.

Even as a young boy, I realized there wasn't a plan, only driving south to get as far away as possible. My dad tried to remain calm, but I could tell he was panicking, and he would do anything to get away. That night in a hotel room in North Carolina, while watching television, my pop's picture came across the screen, along with several other members of the J.B.M. who weren't apprehended in the FBI's pre-dawn raids, as wanted fugitives who were believed to have fled the Philadelphia area. The FBI and media were appealing to the public for tips on the whereabouts of these wanted fugitives.

My mom called later that night to check in, especially on me. After speaking with my dad, he handed me the phone so I could talk to her. She asked me if I was okay. I told her that I was fine. She began crying telling me that she misses me and that she loves me. I told her that I love her too and handed the phone back to my dad. I could hear her through the phone when I gave the phone back to my dad saying, *"Bae, don't let anything happen to my baby."* My dad assured her that he wouldn't let anything happen to me.

Looking back, I feel like he said that to her out of reaction, when in truth, he didn't know what he would do if the FBI caught up with us. This was the first time in my life that I saw fear in my dad's face and eyes.

Sensing the gravity of the situation, my dad called one of my uncles to find a legitimate attorney. As I listened to my pop and the others talk, I was in a fog, dazed over everything that was happening. One day I was in school, then I was brought home, and then, for the next two and a half weeks, I was on the run with my pop, two other adult men, and my mom's miniature poodle. There was no talk of school, living arrangements, or food.

Finally, we arrived in Georgia. I didn't know what to expect. I only knew that my pop, uncle, and my pop's henchman were working to acquire new licenses and passports to assume new identities. And then, just like that, with no rhyme or reason, we were going to turn around and head back up I-95 to go home. What I didn't know at the time was that my Uncle Tone, my father's brother, Lil Tony's dad had secured a lawyer for my dad, and the lawyer said it would be best if my dad turned himself in.

Before we departed for home, my pop sat me down and told me, *"It is time for you to be a man. I don't know if you know what's going on, but I have to go back to turn myself in. You are going to have to step up and keep an eye on your mother and brother for me."* He also explained to me about the Byard Brothers from West Philly, who would be coming into our neighborhood blazing when they found out he had turned himself in. *"We have been beefing with them,"* my pop said. *"And I know they will come now because the team is down, so be on point!"*

About five days later, my pop met with an attorney, Stephen Patrizio, at his Center City office. They headed to the federal courthouse at 7th & Market Streets in Philadelphia so my pop could turn himself in. As predicted, the Byard Brothers were on Douglas Street
that night, shooting up the block and shouting, *"Where they at now?"* The baton had been passed to me by my dad to do

whatever was necessary to protect my family, so amidst the shooting, I walked around with no fear, shouting, *"Give me a hammer[3]; they are shooting at my people."* Even the metal green and white awning on Grem's front porch had bullet holes in it. With guns blazing and bullets flying, the embryonic stage of the wolf's birth was expedited on Douglas Street that night.

With my pop now in prison, in addition to being charged with protecting my mom and older brother, at the age of 13, I was commissioned to collect debts from dozens of people who owed my pop; however, no one paid, giving one excuse after another why they didn't have the money. I knew I had to man up and get this done. My cousin Luck had owed my dad a few bucks from his time hustling[4] for him, and after speaking with him during a call home from prison, Luck agreed to give some work[5] to my mom.

With half an ounce of crack cocaine from Luck, my mom knew she had to sell it and it would net her nearly $1,000. She decided to give the half ounce to someone else to sell for her on consignment. But the guy burned[6] her, so she told me that I needed to go and get her money! She gave

---

[3] Hammer—slang for gun
[4] Hustling—code for selling drugs
[5] Work—slang for drugs
[6] Burned —slang for not paying up

me a fully loaded 9mm Ruger, which previously belonged to my pop, to take care of the situation and get her money.

Having held a gun many times when I was younger, something felt different about this gun. It was something about the size of the gun, along with the cold, hard steel, that gave me a feeling of power. Putting the gun in my waist, I felt like God. There was a euphoric yet powerful, and unstoppable feeling that rushed over me. The adrenaline rushing through me felt like nothing I had ever felt before.

After a brief search, I found the guy who had burned my mom. Rather than shoot him, I pistol-whipped him repeatedly, causing him to fall to the ground covered in blood. I was able to get $130 out of the guy's pockets after I ran through[7] them while he was down, and then the guy got up and ran.

When I returned and reported to my mom what had happened and gave her the $130, she said, *"You dumb ass. You don't ever leave anybody alive. You don't leave somebody alive to be able to come back and retaliate on you. If you pull a gun on anyone, you better use it,"* she screamed. *"I thought you were a man!"* I said it would never happen again, telling her, *"I will put their lights out from now on, Mom."* She reminded me that it was about keeping my dad's name alive and sending a message.

---

[7] Ran through—slang for rummaging

Despite our differences, I still coveted my mom's love and approval. She was someone that people on our block looked up to. A social butterfly, she always dressed well and acted as if she was all-knowing and in control.

My cousin Luck gave my mom more work, a half ounce, and this time she gave it all to me to sell. And that's how it all began. As a 13-year-old, I bagged it as nickel rock bags and made $1400. The wolf was officially born.

What can easily be perceived as a person taking the easy way out is that person's means of survival. As humans, we all have an innate ability to survive, however, some place limits on their means of survival while others do not. Neither individual is right or wrong in their quest for survival, they just want to survive.

Rafiq Williams

Chapter III The Corner

After 8th grade, it was time to choose a high school and I enrolled at George Washington High School. I soon discovered that GW wasn't a "basketball school," so I wanted to transfer to Simon Gratz. To transfer, I had to have a parent's signature. My pop was in prison and my mom had kicked me out. I had to pay my mom $500 to sign the transfer papers. My mom always saw an opportunity to make money, and this was no different; she was a natural hustler. I don't even know how she arrived at $500 for her signature.

Initially, I felt that was too high for her signature, and was leaning towards not paying that amount. I quickly realized that I needed her to accomplish what I wanted, and this was a life lesson for me, that nothing was free and you get what you pay for. Gratz had a highly-ranked basketball program, and I thought I would be the school's star player. But I soon discovered that you had to be a real, dedicated athlete to compete. I signed up for the team, and practices started.

At one of the first practices, the players had to run from Gratz to Kelly Drive and back, which was about three to five miles. I was thinking, and we're going to run where? Is there going to be some sort of transportation? But I followed suit after the other players and I started to jog. I looked around and saw that no one was following us, so I stopped and then jogged a bit more.

When we returned to the gym, somehow the coach, Bill Ellerby, a highly respected teacher and coach, told me exactly where I had stopped. He then sent me home for the day without ever stepping foot onto the court. In my mind, I'm thinking to myself that this dude must be crazy for sending me home without even getting a chance to ball! The next day I showed up late to practice, Coach Ellerby pulled me aside and said, *"I don't think you are quite ready for Simon Gratz basketball. You can come back next year."*

My ego was shot, and I was embarrassed, but like always, I didn't show it. While I was embarrassed at first, I then became upset with myself for messing up my own goals because of my foolishness and, quite frankly, arrogance. I knew I really couldn't blame anyone but myself, but that didn't stop me from trying to blame Coach Ellerbee.

Far too often as teenagers, we never want to accept responsibility for our actions. It always has to be someone else's fault. I stayed in school until November of that year. Every time I saw the basketball coach in school, I ducked and went the other way. Again, not ready to face the reality of my own blown opportunity. The coach represented failure, and I was not accustomed to failure on any level.

As I thought about the missed basketball opportunity, I also began thinking about how much money I was missing from the streets by being in school. Yet I was conflicted knowing how my mother felt about school and getting an education. But I also knew that if I was going to survive, I needed to be on the streets.

The conflict was settled and in a matter of weeks, I decided to dedicate myself to hustling full-time. I started earning $2500-3000 a day, but my net take after expenses was only about $700. The bulk of this money had to go to the person giving me the drugs. Ignorance leads many in this line of work to overlook the overhead as if all their earnings would be theirs. The ultimate goal is to surpass your boss and begin working for yourself and supply the other young or older dealers who want to come up[8].

My reliability on the corner established me as a go-to dealer. At 13, I was able to purchase my first car for $275, a white Chevy Citation from my cousin Bern. There were a couple of drawbacks with the car. It couldn't drive faster than 45 mph due to a slipping transmission, had a busted windshield, but you couldn't tell me that I wasn't the man with this car. Not to mention this would be my first time driving. However, as with everything in my life to this point, I found a way, and I just figured I would do it. After

---

[8] Want to come up—make money

all, I had watched my brother Mike drive our mom's car. I thought to myself, how hard could driving be? Parking was a challenge for me, so I would only park in spots I could pull into. I practiced driving on the streets late at night so no one would see me. I used fake stickers for inspection stickers and parked on Cumberland or Douglas Street. Ironically, I didn't have an official driver's license for another 14 years, finally getting one when I was 27.

I was now living in an abandoned house owned by my pop with my 40-year-old uncle, Grem's younger brother, Butch, who was also known as BL. BL was who we went to hide out with in Georgia when my pop was on the run from the FBI. The FBI was supposed to have seized this house when my pop's properties were confiscated, but somehow it was missed.

The house did not have electricity, running water, a working bathroom, or a kitchen. Uncle Butch would go to Grem's house to get a gallon jug of water, and we got soap and deodorant from a neighborhood store. I learned how to take bird baths, simply washing under my arms, my private parts, and my butt, and called it a day. A plastic bag-lined bucket served as our toilet. This was night and day from how I had just lived prior. It was a harsh reality.

From time to time, BL and I occasionally rented a room at the Days Inn on Roosevelt Boulevard so we could get a good night's sleep and a warm shower. I had a few clothes that I kept in a black trash bag.

BL, a heroin addict, would go to Grem's house to wash our clothes. Grem would have gladly opened her home to me but only if I would relinquish selling drugs. Me and BL used a kerosene heater to keep warm and survived on Doritos, hot sausages, and Oodles of Noodles. We would cook our noodles on the kerosene heater with a pot that we got from the Thrift Store. We would warm up our sausages on the kerosene heater if
they got cold. They were usually hot when we bought them from the neighborhood gas station.

Living on the streets was hard, very hard, I cried many nights but no one ever knew it. To mask the pain, I played around with cough syrup with codeine and weed. Luckily, despite dabbling in drugs, I never became addicted.

My dad's reach was never far away, telling me, *"You out there selling drugs, and you are not taking care of us. Pay the car notes!"* Ever dutiful and continually seeking my pop's approval and love, I would give my mom the money to pay the car loans. Except the loans were never paid. I learned that both of the family cars were repossessed. I suspected that my mom chose to use the money to maintain her lifestyle rather than pay the loans.

Most people didn't know my mom was addicted to drugs because she always wore high-end clothing. She always had money to show her friends a good time, so who would suspect that someone who was living like this was addicted to drugs? Most of us hold the image of someone with bad teeth, dirty clothes, and unkempt hair as someone whose addicted to drugs. Life has taught me that some rich people are, and were, equally as addicted as others that I knew, but they had the money to cover up their addiction.

I was experiencing a range of emotions. I got to do what I wanted when I wanted with this new freedom of living on my own. I was able to be me, and I was the boss of me. But as time continued to move on, I was constantly reminded of my new reality. It was cold outside, really cold, and at times my feet were nearly frostbitten due to the kerosene heater running out of fuel in the middle of the night.

The emotion that seemed to overtake me was one of despair. How did I get here? How much longer would this current state of living last? Then my mind would shift to motivation, this was not going to be the state of my life forever. Grem always told me I needed to survive; sometimes, she would feed me. But because of my stubbornness and pride, I wouldn't ask for help.

I had a very strong willpower and a sense of self-preservation. If I was going to survive, I had to do it on my own, my way. I was destined to prove to my mom that I didn't need her or anyone and that I would survive. I returned to my corner on Douglas and Cumberland to shoot dice, smoke weed, and talk to the neighborhood girls. And I continued to sell drugs.

That street corner, my strip 33rd and Cumberland Street to 31st and Cumberland, helped make me into a bona fide dope boy. Someone who earned the respect of all the people in the area. I earned my street name on that corner, Cube, after the notoriously famous rapper Ice Cube from NWA. (Only my nickname was given in response to Ice Cube's character, Doe Boy, in the Boyz in the Hood movie).

While I was building success in the game, I decided to return to school the following September after having dropped out in November of 9th grade. When I arrived at the high school office, they said I was in 10th grade, and they gave me a 10th-grade roster. I didn't question it; jumping a grade was fine by me. But my school days were short-lived as the streets continued to call me and high school became secondary to survival. If I was going to survive, I needed to be dedicated to the streets, dedicated to hustling, so I dropped out again. Mentally, I tried to shape the image of what I thought I should be doing by age 14. I had responsibilities, and people depended on me.

I was on my corner, spending many of my waking hours there. I could be out at all times of the night, as I had nowhere to go. I also began messing around with one particular teenage girl, Shaunda, 19, who was five years older than me, and she already had a six-month-old son. She had graduated from Ben Franklin High School the previous year, so I told her I was 17. After all, I had a car and was able to stay out all night. We partied hard and often, and within a short time, about six months, Shaunda became pregnant.

When my mom found out, she told Shaunda that I was only 15 and that she could have her arrested. Shaunda was shocked to find out my real age as she said I certainly didn't behave in any way like a 15-year-old. I was angry with my mom for telling Shaunda my real age, I told my mom, *"That's why I can't stand you, and it's why I don't live with you now."* I had been helping take care of Lionell, whom I nicknamed Arti later in life, Shaunda's baby, as my son, since I was 14 as Lionell's father was absent.

It was ironic that as someone who never really experienced childhood, I became a father twice over at 16 with the birth of my first biological child. We named him Rafiq Williams Jr., whom we nicknamed Rowdy due to his behavior. Truthfully, I had never really wanted to have kids as I didn't think I would live to see my 18th birthday. It was 1994, and my dad was granted a new trial when he won his appeal and was sent home.

This was a happy time for most of my family, but for me it was awkward.

When my dad went away, I was a young boy who was conflicted on who he wanted to be. Now I was nearly 17, and in my eyes I'm a man. Living life on the street forced me to grow up extremely fast. My dad came home to two grandchildren I fathered, one on the way, and one my brother Mike had fathered. He was on house arrest pending the outcome of his new trial. He subsequently was found not guilty after his new trial. He was a free man with no barriers.

Any person who doesn't have hope for a better today or tomorrow will inevitably engage in reckless, harmful, or criminal behavior.

Rafiq Williams

Chapter IV Locked Up

With two sons and now a daughter to support, and other financial responsibilities, I continued to hone my skills on the streets. I would stand on the corner selling drugs, open-air style—out in the open—and someone would walk or ride up to copp.[9] These types of sales are more risky than other methods used because with open-air sales you sell to anyone, including undercover narcotics officers. I did that on an occasion and was arrested shortly after. I was ultimately taken to the 22nd police district at 17th and Montgomery Streets where I was placed in a cell and had to wait to be released to a parent or guardian.

Naturally, my mom was called and she came to the station to have me released. Once we got outside of the station and out of earshot of any police officers, she said, *"You know this is gonna cost you."* I knew what that meant, and asked her, how much? She told me $250, and I said I got you when I get to the block. Once I got to the block, I paid her the money she asked for. That wasn't the end of my open-air style of dealing, let's just say that I was more careful. From that day forward I only sold to fiends[10] that I knew, and didn't sell to any new faces, especially White ones!

---

[9] Copp—buy
[10] Fiends—drug users and addicts

There were also sales when fiends would call my pager, and I would return the call on a pay phone, which was later upgraded to a cell phone, the old, bulky, gray flip Motorola phones. Only a few of us on the strip (block) had these phones. I thought that money equaled success and it would bring me happiness. But over time, I learned that in this line of work, it was all fool's gold. Some neighbors who had watched my brother and me grow up and what we were exposed to, predicted that I would be dead or in jail by the time I was 15. Somehow, I defied those odds, at least for a while.

Shaunda and my three children were living in a house a block over, on Natrona Street, near the main strip. I was still living a hard life on the streets and in the abandoned house, but she would let me spend the night from time to time. I also aspired to be the one people would look to if they had a problem, any problem. I was young and reckless, I frequently rode around the city with a pound of weed to smoke every day, and inevitably I had run-ins with the law.

As a teenager, my homie, Umar, along with my old head[11], Mani, and I were pulled over by the law for running a red light near the Philadelphia Art Museum. I was in the back seat when we got in a high-speed chase on Kelly Drive.

---

[11] Old Head—older male with street cred

By 33rd and Girard Ave, the cops surrounded us, broke the driver-side window, pulled Umar out through the window, and slammed him to the ground. Mani was pulled out of the passenger seat and slammed to the ground. Then I heard a cop say, "Don't act like you sleep now," and pulled me out of the car from the back seat where I was pretending to be asleep. They pulled me through the front side car window and slammed me to the ground, too. The three of us were immediately handcuffed and placed in the back of a paddy wagon.[12]

The initial cop that saw Umar run the light said, *"I saw them throw something out of the window,"* and went back to look for it along with a couple of other officers. The cops located the guns we had thrown out of the window during the chase. Both guns were 9mm, one was chrome and the other was black. All three of us were taken to the police station where Umar readily confessed to owning the guns after Mani had coaxed him to take the case, and I was able to escape being charged and prosecuted.

In another encounter, my friend Riq and I were pulled over by the law at 22nd & Dolphin Streets while driving a four-door, red Olds Delta 88 with tinted windows. Unbeknownst to the approaching officer we had guns in the car. The 12-gauge was under the back seat, and the Tec-9

---

[12] Paddy wagon—transport vehicle

was under the front passenger seat within reach of Riq. I had a 10mm Smith & Wesson tucked in my waistband. We had been riding around smoking weed as usual.

As we rolled down the windows to rap with the cop, smoke from the weed rushed out of the windows. This caused the cop to back up, cough, and say, *"Damn!"* But in that same instance, the cop heard shots fired nearby. He rushed back to his car and let Riq and me off without so much as a warning, but he did say, *"Today y'all lucky day"*. Not to mention, I didn't have a driver's license, but neither did many people driving in my hood at that time.

Then there was the fall night in 1993 when my brother Miz, (nickname for Mike when he got older), said he had been sent home from the Navy for smoking weed. Having Miz home was a chance for us to buss it up[13] and chill with each other again. Secretly, I missed my brother and wished on many nights that he was there with me on those streets. I mean he was my older brother and at times my protector, but there was no Miz, just me.

We caught up with our cousin Luck and homie Riq, jumped into Luck's car, and headed to the Clam Bar in South Philly. It was known for good seafood and stayed open late when other stores were closed. The four of us sat around rappin' about the day's events and what we planned

---

[13] Buss it up—talk

to do once we returned to the block. It was a light-hearted night with laughs. The four of us jumped back into Luck's shiny, burgundy new-looking Acura Legend with chrome rims.

      Miz slid into the driver's seat since he was the only one with a valid driver's license. This made the most sense, knowing that the law who patrolled the Clam Bar area was notorious for pulling over black people who drove nice cars. Within minutes, the Acura was surrounded by cops. A police sergeant came to the car window with his gun drawn. Miz handed the sergeant his license, the car's registration, and a fake insurance card. Yes, we had fake insurance cards. When you're in the game you can get anything, for a price.

      The sergeant took the stuff Miz handed him and went back to his car. Once the cop ran his license, he realized Miz was AWOL from the Navy. Miz had left the military without permission knowing that me, his younger brother, and cousin were making a lot of money on the streets, and he had had enough of the structured life in the Navy, earning peanuts. He envisioned himself hitting the block and hustling with the fam. But as it would turn out later, Miz was lousy at it. The cops arrested Miz, who ultimately served three months in the brig, in Connecticut. Once again, I was able to escape.

Several years later, a tense situation evolved on a warm summer night in August 1997 when my mom came by in her red Firebird. She was sitting in her car and talking with Miz and me, who had been released from the brig. I noticed a dude walking through my neighborhood who shouldn't be there. Earlier that week, that same dude had robbed me at gunpoint, but he had been wearing a mask. He didn't think I would be able to identify him because of the mask, but I was able to identify him from his voice. The reason that I knew what he sounded like was because I had smoked weed with him on several occasions. He was friends with a friend of mine, Tooby Joe.

Quickly, I told my mom to leave. She responded, *"Boy, don't tell me to leave, I leave when I'm ready. I'm your mom."* Suddenly, I started letting it fly[14] at the guy walking through my neighborhood, and my mom began screaming hysterically. I shot the dude in his hip and chest. I guess you could say that I traumatized my mom that day. The law eventually came, but by then, I was gone, and so was the dude, Chris, who I had shot multiple times. A friend of the shooting victim happened to be driving by and saw Chris on the ground. He put Chris in his car and drove him to the hospital. Miz gave me a look of surprise and adoration simultaneously because he was no longer looking

---

[14] Letting it fly—shooting

at the little brother whom he left behind many years ago. You could say that day I became his big brother.

The next day after successful surgery to remove the bullets and stop the bleeding, Chris tried to blackmail me, telling me through a message that was relayed to me by a mutual friend, Sasquatch, that he would report the shooting to the law if I didn't give him $5,000. I was not deterred from telling him that his family would spend $5,000 on his funeral if he went to the law, so I told him to choose. Chris sent word to me, by this same mutual friend who delivered the first message, that it was cool, meaning he would leave the situation alone, opting to stay alive. Once again, I escaped a more serious encounter with the law.

A year later, in October 1998, I was home, or I should say at my baby mom's house at Lawrence and Huntingdon Streets, located in an area known as the "Badlands". This was a section of Philly that was close to Kensington. I lived there with my girlfriend, Shaunda, and our three children, already having two sons. My beautiful baby girl Shanyia, whom we nicknamed Nya, was born in 1995, 10 months after Rowdy and a few years before the move to the Badlands.

My luck in escaping the law had come to an end. We were awakened by the ringing of the phone at 6:05 in the morning, it was my Grem. The S.W.A.T. Team had raided her house on Douglas Street that morning searching for me.

Grem warned me that they were coming for me. I could hear the fear in her voice as she told me. Back in 1975, my uncle Jimmy, her son, was killed by the cops, and she didn't want the same thing to happen to me. She began crying, but I didn't have time to console her, so I hung up the phone and thought about my next move.

I had been identified by someone as the shooter in a murder that occurred on Stanley and Huntingdon Streets two months prior. Grem's house was only about 15 minutes away, so I knew time was of the essence. However, I thought I had time because no one, except for one person, knew where we lived in the Badlands.

That one person was Shaunda's mom, and I didn't think the cops knew about her, but boy was I wrong. They did go there and Shaunda's mom told the cops where we lived out of fear from the threats the cops were making towards Shaunda and our children. They told her that they would see to it that the kids were taken from Shaunda and that she would be arrested if she didn't tell them where we lived. They left two cops at Shaunda's mom's house to ensure that she wouldn't call and tip us off.

Sensing the urgency to bounce I stood up quickly and started running through the house, throwing clothes into a small bag. I was preparing to head to the Greyhound Bus Terminal in Center City on 10th and Arch Streets, about 10 miles from my house. I had no idea where I was heading, but I knew I had to leave. I heard my two pit bulls barking, so I knew somebody was close to the house, as this was the only time they usually barked. I went to the window and peeked through the blinds and saw a paddy wagon riding by with cops looking and pointing at my house. I knew this was it, it must be the cops looking for me, and now they were just outside my door.

Without hesitation, I sprinted out of the house trying to hold on to what felt like the last minutes of my freedom. I kicked open an alley door on the other side of my yard leading to Orkney Street, hoping to avoid capture. But there they were, the law, all of whom were Black; they had both ends of the alley covered. When I emerged, the cops, two plainclothes cops, and four S.W.A.T. officers had guns drawn to both sides of my head. They threw me to the ground. One cop pulled a picture out, placed it next to my face, and said, *"Yeah, that's him."* And with that, they cuffed me tightly. When they pulled me to my feet, the cuffs tightened around my wrists even more.

Once I was apprehended, the cops called for a paddy wagon. Walking to the wagon slowly, I thought to myself, damn, they got me, this is the end. I didn't even get a chance to tell my kids that I love them. I thought for sure that I would never see them again, except behind a plastic partition if my baby's mom brought them to see me.

Two months before my arrest, I was on the block when the nephew of one of my homies, Raheem, came to get me. Raheem had got burned in a dice game, and he wanted to fight the guy who burned him. As the problem fixer, I was ready to help. Raheem jumped onto the back of my motorcycle, a blue Suzuki 1000 that I just got a few weeks earlier, and we raced off to Stanley and Huntingdon Streets, less than two minutes away.

As we approached, a young boy named Bug Eyes was standing in the street and pulled out his shotgun. When Bug Eyes saw it was me, he said, *"Whoa, I didn't know he went to get you, Cube. We good!"* I told Bug Eyes that Raheem wanted a fair one. Bug Eyes said cool, and he and Raheem started rumbling. When it became clear that Bug Eyes was winning, Bug Eyes and I agreed they were good, and they stopped. Raheem and I jumped back on my motorcycle and took off. As we were leaving, shots were fired in our direction. Raheem said, *"They shooting at us!"* I said, *"That ain't got nothing to do with me,"* and we sped away. Later that night, I heard that an innocent bystander had been shot and killed. At some point, someone alleged that it was me, that I had returned and was the shooter. So here I am, being arrested at gunpoint, handcuffed, and shoved into a paddy wagon.

Not having any confidence in the legal system, I chose to remain silent, which was my right, while I was in custody. After my arrest, I was taken to Hahnemann Hospital because of sore ankles and wrists from being taken into custody. Next, I was carted off to the Police Administration Building, called the Round House at 8th and Race Streets.

I was put in a cell and told that detectives wanted to speak with me. The next stop was the interrogation room, where the air conditioner was on full blast, this is usually done to make suspects uncomfortable. I told the detectives that I had not received my Miranda rights and asked for a lawyer before they attempted to begin their hour-long line of questioning. The detectives left, and I was left alone for the next five hours in that freezing-cold interrogation room.

The detectives finally returned for another hour of questioning, which they weren't supposed to do because I asked for a lawyer after they had executed a search warrant on Shaunda's house. The detectives questioned me about a gun, a black .45-caliber Smith and Wesson, they found at Shaunda's house under the cushion of a living room chair that was near the front door. I said nothing.

A different black detective who was now questioning me was holding that gun, cocking it, and de-cocking it, and he said, *"Why didn't you grab this when you were running out? I wish you would have reached for this, and then we could have killed your black ass!"* Again, I said nothing. He was looking to get a rise out of me and begin running my mouth, but I continued my silence. The part where they say that whatever you say can be used against you is very true, that I knew from my old heads, who had previously schooled me on any run-ins with the law.

I had been there for more than seven hours without an opportunity to use a bathroom or even have a glass of water, but what they didn't know is that I have endured harsher environments and ridicule, so this treatment and their comments weren't effective. Cheese sandwiches and bitter tea were usually given to detainees at the police station at very specific times, but it was more than two days before I would get anything to eat.

I was escorted downstairs and was placed in a holding cell to wait for a bail hearing. I was there for 36 additional hours waiting for my name to be called to see the bail commissioner. Finally, I was called, and I heard the bail commissioner say, *"$50,000 for attempted murder and W.O.B for the homicide."* I waited all that time just to be told that I wouldn't be going anywhere which they could've told me earlier. That's when I learned that two people had been shot that night in August, and only one had survived.

I was returned to the holding cell, and then eight other men and I were transported by paddy wagon to the Curran-Curran-Fromhold Correctional Center (CFCC) on

State Road in Philadelphia. After arriving, we were taken to the receiving room, where we were each searched thoroughly. The smell in the receiving room was unlike anything that I ever smelled.

Understand that the receiving room housed over a hundred men or more who hadn't showered in days. Not to mention the addicts mixed in with us who were going through withdrawal, which meant plenty of vomiting and diarrhea. The eight to ten holding cells at the jail had a single bench and see-through doors that slid open, and once again, the room temperature was freezing. There were about 12 men or more in each holding cell.

Next, we were each given a clear identification wristband and ushered by a guard into the shower. We were never alone for even a second. After the shower, I was given an orange jumpsuit and, from there, sent to quarantine for up to 30 days waiting for clearance from any communicable diseases.

While in quarantine, the rooms stank from pungent odors from the inmates not having deodorant and again the smell of drug addicts detoxing, and going through withdrawal by vomiting or from continuous trips to the toilet with diarrhea. Even though the bathrooms were located inside the respective cells where we slept, the disgusting smells permeated the entire area.

I spent my time in quarantine alone as much as possible. I was still trying to make sense of being locked up, and I certainly didn't trust anyone. I knew it was vital that I remain focused and on point to feel out my new environment. I wasn't there to make new friends. There was a small rec yard, which no one used because they didn't have anything to use in the yard since we were all recently housed there.

Most of the inmates spent their time on the phones trying to communicate with their loved ones, begging them to pay their bail or get them a lawyer. They were desperate to get out. One minor distraction was the television in the dayroom, where most people would congregate. I thought they watched some of the dumbest shows, such as COPS. I couldn't figure out why inmates would want to spend their time watching shows about police arresting other people while they were incarcerated. Interest in those television shows always baffled me. I never took the time to indulge in watching television for entertainment, at least not initially.

Our meals were served in a dining area on the unit. Following the quarantine, I was given a set of blues, shirts, and pants, and taken to the general population. No more orange jumpsuits unless you were in the visiting room. I remember the C.O. trying to instill fear in us by saying, "*I hope y'all are ready because this is where it goes down, good luck.*" The wolf in me was on full display now after that comment from the C.O. This would be my home for the next five years.

If a person isn't careful, a place that was intended for rehabilitation can transform them into something worse than the individual they were when they entered that environment. An old head, John, once told me that if I have 10 negative friends, I am bound to be number 11.

Rafiq Williams

Chapter V Doin' Your Bid

I thought to myself, I can't believe that I am actually in prison about to find out what cell I would be in once I was assigned a unit. I was carrying a bedsheet and a blanket as I looked around slowly above and below me. I took a deep breath and realized that life just got real for me. Here I am 21 years old and I have just been sent to jail for murder and attempted murder.

There is a distinct difference between jail and prison. Jail is where you get sent while awaiting trial if you are unable to post bail, or like in my situation, you didn't receive bail. Prison is where you go once you are convicted and receive a sentence. So much stuff happens in jail due to the amount of turnover that takes place daily. Most inmates walk around frustrated ready to burst at the slightest indiscretion, dispute, or sign of disrespect. We made makeshift knives out of pretty much anything we could get our hands on. These weapons are referred to as whacks in jail.

My wolf persona was on full display when I entered my cell block. I observed guys doing pull-ups on the second-floor tier and guys in the day room wearing doo-rags. I kept trying to focus on everything around me while the C.O. was telling me to step up. I looked over my shoulder, thinking about everything I had heard about jail from my old heads back on the block. It wasn't that I was really scared, I was just tense and, maybe, a little anxious. But one thing I knew for sure, there was no time to be scared or fearful. I knew that on the streets, people could smell fear. Even the slightest hint of fear in jail could be far worse. I also knew I would have to jack up my wolf persona. I knew that my experience of working and living on the streets would help me now as I thoroughly surveyed my new surroundings.

With authority, I said to the C.O., *"Show me where my room is. Who will I be cellies with?"* If the C.O. heard me, she didn't acknowledge the question. We just kept walking. Finally, we came to a cell, and she said, *"Williams, this is your cell."* I peered inside and took a step back. I told the C.O., *"You're not putting me in there! I lived with a dope fiend before, and I am not going to stand for it in here!"* I told the C.O. I couldn't do certain things, and living with a dope-addicted cellmate, someone who would be vomiting frequently and having other physical, debilitating issues, was not one of them. The C.O. slowly looked me over and said, *"Let me see what I can do."* I could hear my grandpop, Ray Ballenger saying, *"If you don't stand for something, then you will fall for anything."* I wasn't about to fall for being cellies with a dope fiend for one minute.

The C.O.s were street savvy, too. When they looked me over, they knew I had been someone out on the streets.

It was all in the way that I carried myself and the authority with which I spoke to her. Like I said, some people fall for anything, and I wasn't one of those people. As I waited for the C.O., I took a deep breath, looked around, and thought, how did this happen? I knew I wanted something different in my life, but I didn't know how to get it. And what was worse, I didn't think it was attainable. Street life was all I knew. But I wasn't on the streets anymore, and I also knew that I had to figure out what stance I would need to take now that I was on the inside. Did I need to be a wolf in overdrive, or would I need to tone it down?

Initially, I observed different cliques of men, I was trying to determine which ones thought they were running things on the cell block. I wondered if I would need to confront anyone, or if I needed to form an alliance with some.

As we continued walking, the C.O. and I moved about four cells down the block and stopped at another cell. My new roommate was a Christian named Cadillac Willy. He was about 65-years old and considered to be an old head. Cadillac Willy was a pimp from New York who had been pulled over by police while driving through Philly. There were multiple warrants out for his arrest.

When we first met, he was waiting to be extradited to New York. I moved in, and I realized that Cadillac Willy reminded me of my Uncle BL, with whom I had lived in the abandoned house. Except Cadillac Willy wasn't hooked on drugs. He was chill, talkative, and very knowledgeable. He helped me craft my view of jail life and how I could do my time. Cadillac Willy would always say, *"Fiq do the time, don't let the time do you."* I respected him. The problem was that I only lasted on the cell block for two weeks.

The wolf was out, and on the prowl, I was who I was already. Sometimes a fight would occur among the inmates just watching T.V., generally, fights were the result of some form of retaliation for some indiscretion that happened earlier in the day.

One afternoon, an altercation occurred in the multipurpose room with me and other inmates, one of whom was my homie, Bam. The fight was over using a makeshift phone that we had made a few days earlier from a telephone cord that was stolen from the social worker's office and the keypad from a broken landline. Using a piece of shaved metal from a door post, me and Bam stomped and stabbed the offending inmate multiple times in the neck after he had pulled a whack on us.

This dude stomped and crushed the makeshift phone we made because we didn't let him use it. I mentioned before that when wolves sense danger they will neutralize the threat until the threat is no more, so the dude asked for it. No other inmates dared to involve themselves in my altercation, but they did warn me that the C.O.s were on their way. The C.O.s broke up the fight after about five minutes by spraying us with pepper spray, but not before the dude, who had crushed the phone, received multiple stab wounds. Bleeding heavily, he was sent to the infirmary for dozens of stitches.

For my part in the stabbing, I was sent to the hole. There was no discussion about what happened, who started it, or why. On my way to the hole, Cadillac Willy gave me his Bible. *"You're going to need to read something while you are down there,"* he said. I mentioned to him that I was Muslim, and he asked me if I had anything else to read. I said no, and he replied, then you better take this, trust me you will need it. I was grateful that he was trying to look out for me. I didn't know what to expect as I was headed to the hole. By the time I was released from the hole, Cadillac Willy had been extradited to New York, and I never saw him again.

The hole was a small room that was cold and was about 8 x 10 feet with a very small window several feet high off the ground. I was going to be confined there for the next 180 days, 23 hours a day. Everything was contained in one room, my bed, which was similar to those on the cell blocks, a metal slat with a thin mat for a mattress, a toilet, and a metal table were in the room. I was given one hour each day to shower and go outside, where I could exercise or just walk around the tiny jail yard attached to the cell block.

I made good use of my small rectangular window, observing the comings and goings of prison life and watching as some inmates went to church on the nights that church services were called. The only human contact I had was with other inmates who were in the hole and had one hour of outside privileges.

I spent my time in the hole immersed in reading the Bible, and unbeknownst to me a slow transformation from Islam to Christianity began to occur. Grem had always tried to tell me about her God. When I had called home one day to tell her I would need money for a lawyer she said, *"I don't have any money to give you, but I have something much more valuable, something that is worth more than silver or gold, a caring God."* I'm thinking to myself, here she goes with this Jesus stuff again. I'm facing the death penalty and in need of a good lawyer and she's talking about Jesus! I had no interest or belief in her God before I went to jail, but that never stopped her from trying to educate me on her God.

Grem was one to never miss an opportunity to talk about the Lord, and knowing that I was in the hole with no distractions was no different for her. She seized her opportunity to share the Lord with me, sensing that I was weak, like a boxer knows when their opponent is weak and on the verge of going down. Something stuck, but I just didn't know it at the time. As the long days in the hole passed, slowly, my transformation to Christianity began to take shape. It wasn't one specific thing that caused my transformation, it was a combination of things coming together like pieces of a puzzle.

One morning around breakfast, a C.O. stopped outside my cell in the hole where I had been for the last six months. He told me to pack it up, I was getting out of the hole. I looked up and was elated. Finally, I was getting out. I had a vague idea of what month it was. When I was outside for my hour of physical activity, I would always ask the C.O. the day and date. Usually, the C.O. replied sarcastically, *"Why? Are you going somewhere?"* I decided not to keep track of the months in the hole because I felt it would have driven me crazy. Just getting the information from the C.O. would be less painful. When I emerged from the hole, my transformation to Christianity had been completed.

I was escorted to a cell block that had an available bed, D2-2. My new cellie was Lil Boo, who had been federally indicted for possession of a kilo of cocaine, along with state charges for murder. He was also from the streets and we had a beef with one another. Several years before, it had been reported to me, through the back channels of street life, that Lil Boo had been responsible for the death of my close homie, John L. Lil Boo looked at me and asked, *"We good?"* I thought long and hard. I told him, *"Whatever had happened out on the streets is going to stay on the street. I am going to accept you for who you are."* This was my opportunity to live out my new faith by demonstrating forgiveness.

One night after we had been cellies for some time and had shared a few meals he opened up to me about the death of my homie John L. He told me about all of the events leading up to his murder, which were in line with everything I knew already, and shockingly he told me who killed John L. It was someone that I had heard of before, and suspicions were surrounding this dude for years, but we couldn't prove anything without an actual witness, and Lil Boo was that witness. Now everything made sense! In time, me and Lil Boo developed a good relationship.

On my new cell block, I continued to read the Bible and even led Bible study groups with a few other inmates. The C.O.s only permitted a few inmates in another's cell at one time, but they would make an exception for us. A few C.O.s would even join us in prayer. As a small group, we would read a chapter from the books in the Bible and discuss what we read. I witnessed changes in some inmates who participated in the Bible studies. Even Muslims, at times, would stop by my cell early in the morning before going to court and ask me to pray for them. I would attend church services twice weekly, one for an hour and the other for 90 minutes.

Services were always crowded, but not just for religious reasons. Many inmates would use this time to get off the block or meet friends who they don't get to regularly see. It was common for co-defendants to meet there who were intentionally separated to prevent them from game planning for their trials. It was also a time to pass knives, drugs, and cigarettes, as the C.O.s wouldn't interrupt or monitor the services. It was an opportunity for some to hurt someone for perceived and actual physical threats but controlled themselves enough to let it ride until they saw the person somewhere else. We may have been serving the Lord, but it would have been very bad for anyone who brought violence into our church service.

For me, the services were a time for conversations and closeness with Jesus. I was not interested in getting involved in any foolishness, I kept my mind on the Lord. I held two jobs after being released from the hole, working on the unit cleaning up and serving food and another as a recreation worker in the gym. I often worked a third job in the barber shop, cutting hair. While I had three jobs, I was only paid for one job. Having the other jobs was a way to pay homage to my Grem, who had often reminded me growing up that idle time is the devil's playground.

When it came to socializing with others, I gravitated toward the older inmates, the old heads, as we called them. I followed the unwritten rule that you looked after and respected the old heads unless the older inmate was in for rape, sexual molestation of a child, or committed some crime against another older person. If their sexual crime was revealed, they generally asked for protective custody (PC). If they didn't receive protective custody, they would be sent out of the jail by ambulance immediately, from being stabbed. *If* they survived, then the C.O.s would put them in protective custody even if they objected. Suspects who are brought to jail for high-profile cases are usually put into the hole or PC too.

    I made friends with an old head named John. I walked over to him and asked if he wanted to play chess. John was game to play chess, and with help from the C.O.s, we were able to play in the day room several times a day while the block was locked down. C.O.s are people too, and they take a liking to people as well. When a C.O. took a liking to you, that generally came with extra privileges, nothing illegal. However, some C.O.s would smuggle in contraband for those inmates they liked.

    Inmates weren't generally permitted to stay in the day room for hours, but the C.O.s helped to facilitate the chess games, and our friendship grew. Reflecting on John, I thought, *"Real recognize real, we just do. It's like a scent you give off."* John, who already had served 27 years, was brought down to the jail from an upstate prison because he had his death sentence overturned. Usually, inmates like

John were sent straight to administrative segregation. This is also considered the hole, but you could be housed there for over thirty days. This is where I served my time in the hole. I think John was allowed into the general population due to his age. He was an older man with completely gray hair, like I said, C.O.s are people with feelings too.

John told me that he knew I wasn't like the other inmates. He told me that he was always careful about who he surrounded himself with. *"Listen here, young fella, I don't know what you plan to do when you get out, but if you have 10 negative friends, you are bound to be the 11th."* He told me that he knew I was a smart guy. *"I could tell you have a head on your shoulders. If I could rewind the hands of time, I wish someone would have told me that."* I thought hard about what John had said. You have to watch the company you keep so you don't succumb to the negativity.

John watched me as I processed the information and said, *"You look like you got the answer; you understand what I am telling you"*, he said. *"I knew you would get it."* He also told me that opportunities come to those of a prepared mind. He told me to return to my cell, think about preparing my mind, and return later to tell him what he meant. I took it to mean that mental roadblocks would not allow the mind to see opportunities, even if the opportunity was right in front of you, it could pass right by if you aren't prepared for the opportunity.

Later in life, I would teach the quote about opportunities to my children. John also told me that I should always make time for my children. While I was in jail, my children were living with my girlfriend, their mom, Shaunda in the same house in the Badlands where I had tried to elude capture.

I spent a lot of time in the law clinic researching different case laws that pertained to my case. You would be surprised to know that ninety percent of the inmates don't use the law clinic. This always baffled me! Why not try to familiarize yourself with various laws, and the rules of criminal procedures to assist your lawyer with your defense? I remember my lawyer telling me that I was every lawyer's dream client. Not only did I familiarize myself with the various laws, terminology, and strategies, I actually knew what I was talking about. He jokingly said that I would make a great paralegal one day. That encouraged me and made me remember my dream of becoming a lawyer one day before that dream was shattered by my sixth-grade teacher.

While some inmates fancied themselves as legal minds and called themselves jailhouse lawyers, they were not real lawyers. I stayed far away from them because, all too often, if these jailhouse lawyers learned specific details about an inmate's crime(s), they would call the District Attorney expressing a willingness to testify against the other inmate, as if the inmate had confessed to them, to make a better deal for themselves. Usually, they are referred to as jailhouse snitches. Your cellie has this same potential, that's why it's an unwritten rule to never discuss your case with anyone.

Being in jail met a man's basic needs, three hots and a cot, and for many inmates, it provided new friends, however, it could be extremely lonely for others. Though I met a lot of new people, there were still times when I felt very alone being away from my family and the familiar streets where I grew up. While loneliness wasn't exactly a topic of conversation, there were times when I could see people looking around for some sort of companionship. Others were looking to connect so they could hone their nefarious skills, like drug dealing, murder, or robberies.

Behind prison walls, the network of such opportunities was endless. It was a college for criminals looking to continue their illegal activities once they were released. It was as if you were earning a Master's degree in criminology.

Though basic needs were met, we had to supply or purchase some items from the jail commissary, such as toothpaste and deodorant. We had to purchase soap from the commissary also because the soap the jail supplied had a lot of lye in it. The jail commissary carried various food items besides just hygiene and dental supplies and religious items. It was the packs of clams, tuna fish, Oodles of Noodles, and peanut butter and jelly that were the most bought items. We could shop at the commissary regularly, but only if we had enough money in our jailhouse account.

While I had limited funds in my account, once I got out of the hole, I purchased a radio at the commissary and began listening to Gospel music on an AM station whenever I was in my cell. It wasn't long after that when the commissary stopped selling radios because inmates were using the parts to build tattoo guns.

There are many different kinds of people in jail, so there wasn't a shortage of creative individuals who for whatever reason got involved in crime and or drugs. I saw people make things out of material that you would least expect to be used for an invention, and it worked!!! Now I am not saying that it was healthy, but it didn't stop us from getting tattooed. I got one jailhouse tattoo during my time in jail, it was the name JESUS written in Old English letters on my right forearm.

With all the time that many of us had on our hands, we had nothing but time to be creative. There is a saying that the cemeteries and prisons are full of wasted talent, and I can see where this statement comes from. I witnessed a lot of talented people in the jail. The portraits I had an inmate create would rival some of the world's renowned artists.

An inmate's jailhouse account was established once the inmate left the receiving room and was in quarantine. Usually, any money the individual had when they were arrested was deposited into their account. Any additional deposits were what the inmate earned while working at the jail. The jobs only paid $1.50 per hour, so we had to work long hours to have some discretionary spending power.

Family members and friends could also deposit money into an inmate's account. For me, having money in my jailhouse account was like a sense of freedom so I could purchase whatever I needed or wanted from the commissary. I had asked my mom and my dad to put money into my account, after all, they had helped my brother Miz financially when he was in the brig and college, sending him $50 to $100 a week. For whatever reason, they only offered me an occasional $20. Twenty dollars in the commissary didn't buy much, but I was thankful for whatever they could send.

One of my old head friends on the outside, named Duck, was giving my brother, Mike, hundreds of dollars for my jailhouse account, but my brother kept all the money for himself. I found out when I called Duck to ask him for some money about a month later. He told me he had given my brother hundreds of dollars to put on my account. To help quell the anger I had for my parents and brother, I stopped calling them. My relationship with my brother was severed at that time. I couldn't allow them, or him, to continually upset me and let me down.

Initially, I would still call Shaunda, the mother of my children, but her phone calls were so one-sided, with her complaining about problems she had, expecting me to solve them, as if I could do something about them, so I stopped calling her too. Removing the extra stress that these calls brought me helped me to focus better on life behind the walls and my case. I remember telling them that if I lost my case y'all wouldn't have to worry about me anyway. I was looking at either the death penalty or life in prison, so stopping these calls came easy for me.

As resourceful as I was, working several jobs in the jail, the money in my account was very limited. But one thing I learned at a very early age was how to survive. I knew I needed a plan for more cash. So I began observing and listening to the needs and wants of the inmates. I knew tobacco was in high demand, and C.O.s were bringing it in for a price. I devised a plan to connect with a C.O., and with my cousin Luck on the outside, I knew I could sell tobacco inside.

After watching a specific C.O.'s behavior for weeks, one day, I approached him discreetly, about selling cigarettes, and how much he would charge to bring them in.

Soon cartons of Newport Regulars and Newport 100s became weekly deliveries. I paid $100 for each carton. The guard received his cut when the cigarettes came in and I sold everything. I sold individual cigarettes, Newport Regulars for $5 each or $100 a pack, and Newport 100s for $8 each or $160 a pack. Each carton contained 10 packs of cigarettes. In time, I had a healthy jailhouse account, and increased commissary items, as some inmates paid with commissary items. I was incredibly busy. I had a positive reputation and I earned the respect of most inmates and C.O.s.

  Earning money wasn't my only focus. I signed up for various courses the jail offered including anger management which was taught by a visiting psychologist. I knew that I needed some help with my anger. I needed to hear the information about the causes of anger and ways to mitigate it, but I was unable to apply what I learned at that time. My anger issues ran
too deep and were too much a part of who I was, or so I thought at the time. I consider myself a realist. Whether someone was white or black was irrelevant to me. I trusted my instincts. If someone was real, truly genuine, I could feel it.

  I was deeply motivated when it came to my newly found Christian beliefs. I completed an eight-week correspondence course in Bible studies through a school ministry in Boston and earned a certificate. I had learned about the course by chance after seeing it advertised on the back of a Daily Devotional booklet, called My Daily Bread. As a new believer in Christ, completing the weekly readings and assignments helped provide me with a better understanding of biblical truths.

The course helped me to understand things that were a complicated such as the Holy Trinity. I also gained a better understanding of the sacrifices that Jesus Christ had made for me when he died on the cross.

Before this, I had accepted his death for the sins of everyone as truth, but I did not fully comprehend why. After discovering all these truths and completing the Bible courses it allowed me to have richer conversations with Grem. She was ecstatic to learn of my newfound faith and the knowledge I gained in such a short amount of time.

I remember her saying on many occasions for me to let the Lord change me from the inside out. I didn't fully grasp that at the time, but now I know it to mean God has to change your heart for people to be able to observe a change in you. I still had anger in my heart at the time, and couldn't identify why. In time I would be able to identify why I had anger in my heart.

While I was at the top of my class for navigating the treacherous streets, a fractured, dysfunctional family, and homelessness, I only had an 8th-grade formal education. General Educational Development courses were offered two hours a day for 12-week semesters at the jail. I enrolled in a semester in the spring of 1999, the volunteer GED teacher was a petite, attractive Black woman in her 30s with a nice smile. Many of the inmates in my class would stare, some would even try to holler at her, but she held her own. This didn't seem like her first rodeo, so she navigated the attention very well.

    Thinking back, I remember her soft voice and short hair. My street background made me a true skeptic, but for some reason when this GED teacher spoke, I listened. I excelled in the classes, and with encouragement from her, I continued moving forward to complete the requirements. I was one of 12 inmates who enrolled for class that semester. I was attentive in class and completed all required assignments for subjects such as English, math, and social studies.

    When it came time to take the two-hour GED exams, I felt prepared and confident. I have always been a good test taker dating back to my early school days. The results of the test arrived in a sealed envelope about 30 days later. Anxiously awaiting my score, I was pleasantly surprised to learn that I earned a near-perfect score of 220 out of 225. Only four of the 12 inmates in that semester passed the test but none came close to my score. Again, I could hear my mom's words about education. I was excited to call home this time to tell my mom the news. She told me how happy she was for me, but secretly I felt like she thought it was all for nothing.

I remember my GED teacher coming to me after the scores had been given out and telling me that I was smart. She further emphasized that if I was ever released from jail, I should go to college. I laughed, and she said, *"I'm serious!"* I was surprised to learn that I could attend college with a GED. Her words truly spoke to me. She made me believe in myself as she continually reminded me that I could do something more with my life and that I had the academic tools I needed to be successful.

Coming from the streets, I could smell BS a mile away. Yet I felt the genuineness of her words, her sincerity, she believed in me. She made me feel like I belonged in college. She gave me hope. I trusted and believed every word of what she said. It was her encouragement, her sincerity, and belief in my skills that eventually drove me. With my new-found belief in my intellectual ability and potential for college, for once in my life, I believed I was smart enough to make it. I just didn't know how far.

Through the years...

The siblings, Rafiq and Michael Williams

Age 2

Age 5

Age 7

My Childhood

My Parents, Michael and Yolanda Williams

My maternal grandmom, Elaine Ballenger (Center)

My paternal grandmom, Lula "Grem" Williams (Right)

Micheal Williams, my dad and me

Myself (Left), Cousin Luck (Center), Riq (Right)

K-12 Principal

Rafiq and Shay on their wedding day! **6.3.2023**

Left - Right

Em & M, Arti, Dar, Rowdy, Meatloaf, Nya, Cheytown

Rafiq with his oldest two daughters

God's protection and blessings can manifest themselves when we are going through some of the worst storms in our lives.

Rafiq Williams

Chapter VI The Trial

When I arrived at the prison in 1998, I was a 21-year-old, street-smart, mentally strong, emotionally frozen man with an 8th-grade education. As with all the challenges I faced since I was in elementary school, I assessed situations and always devised a survival plan. Assessing situations was a matter of life or death. Walking into the wrong situation without assessing it and preparing for it could land me in the cemetery.

I didn't make it this far without my instincts. I saw too many people incorrectly assess a situation and they wound up in the morgue. Preparing to defend myself against murder charges was no different, it was life or death.

I had done some research in the prison law library, but I was relying heavily on my attorney, Bernard L. Siegel. Mr. Siegel was a highly regarded criminal defense attorney in the Philadelphia area who also taught at Temple's Law School. Mr. Siegel was a court-appointed attorney who was assigned to my case because of the seriousness of the charges against me. Some might have said that having Mr. Siegel was a stroke of luck, but I saw it as a blessing from God.

Within the first few years of me being locked up, I had nine preliminary hearings. The nine hearings were unusual because according to law, if the Commonwealth doesn't proceed to make a case after three scheduled preliminary hearings, the charges are supposed to get tossed. The preliminary hearing is where the prosecutor presents basic evidence for the judge to decide if the case should move forward to trial.

The judge presiding over my case made the same statement at each of my preliminary hearings when the prosecutor asked for a continuance stating that they weren't ready to proceed, saying he was going to toss the case. However, hearing after hearing, the prosecutors kept telling the judge they were waiting to locate a specific eye witness, a man called Bug Eyes.

After about a year, the prosecutors finally found Bug Eyes walking the streets, illegally in possession of a Tec-9 and he was arrested. Bug Eyes was taken to the Criminal Justice Center where I was awaiting my ninth preliminary hearing to either be tossed or proceed as scheduled.

It was ironic or maybe it was purposeful, but Bug Eyes was placed in the cell next to me. When Bug Eyes saw me, he warned me, *"Tell your lawyer not to question me."* Bug Eyes told me he was arrested with a gun that he thought had a body on it, so he decided to name me in the murder and attempted murder. After hours of grueling questioning and pressure from the police, and looking to save himself, Bug Eyes became a snitch and made a deal. Saying he knew me from the streets, he gave police what they wanted and implicated me in the murder that summer night a year ago.

It was enough to have the judge move my case to trial and get Bug Eyes released. After all of this time, I couldn't understand how the Commonwealth had nine opportunities to present its case. I refused to give in to anger, but I was surprised that this could happen within the judicial system. My case was now headed to trial. I knew I was in for the fight of my life.

Meanwhile, Bug Eyes was free and back on the streets, and he remained actively involved in illegal activities. At one point, Bug Eyes stole a police car and ran over a police officer. Yet somehow, he escaped being arrested and the police were unaware of his involvement in the incident. Fortunately, the police officer who Bug Eyes ran over sustained injuries that were not life-threatening. But several months later in August of 2002, Bug Eyes' luck ran out. He was shot and killed after an altercation with another individual. Once again, the perpetrator escaped and Bug's murder went unsolved.

However, the police did investigate me to see if I had anything to do with orchestrating Bug Eyes' murder interviewing my family members and friends.

Bug Eyes' death meant nothing new for my murder charge. The prosecutors were allowed to use the notes from Bug Eyes' earlier testimony at my preliminary hearing.

Finally, two and a half years after my arrest and the death of their key witness, I went to trial.

Preparing for trial, my attorney, Bernard Siegel, used his 21 pre-emptive strikes during jury selection which were allowed because it was a death penalty case. The jury was composed of four males who were Hispanic and white and six women who were Hispanic, Black, and White. The trial proceeded and lasted about 10 days. I took the stand during the trial and told my side of the story. The prosecutor had his chance to cross-examine me as well. He did everything within his power to get me to display the slightest bit of anger; however, none of his antics worked. I remember my attorney telling me before I agreed to take the witness stand in my defense that the jury isn't supposed to hold it against a defendant for not testifying—but they still do, so it was a no-brainer at that point for me to testify.

My attorney and I were hopeful except for one nagging concern. A juror, originally from West Africa, never looked at me and she acknowledged only the prosecutor when she entered the courtroom with head nods and hellos.

When the case went to the jury, they deliberated for a solid week. During their deliberations, the jury requested that the testimony from Bug Eyes be read back to them, but the judge denied their request. The judge told the jury to use their best recollection of the written testimony. The jury also asked the judge to explain the difference between first-degree murder, third-degree murder, and manslaughter. The judge gave them the differences. At this point, both Mr. Siegel and I thought the jury was trying to compromise and find me guilty of a lesser charge.

When the jury finally returned, the judge asked if they had reached a verdict. The jury foreperson stood and said they could not come to a consensus, and they were hopelessly deadlocked. The judge declared a hung jury. My attorney asked to have the jury polled, each juror said not guilty until they reached the juror originally from West Africa. She voted guilty, still never looking once at me or my attorney. I still felt hopeful and encouraged. I was so close to freedom. I had hoped that the Commonwealth would opt to not retry the case since it had been 11-1 to acquit.

Six months later, I was up for a bail hearing. My Grem made her way to the courthouse for the hearing with one of my favorite desserts, a slice of pineapple cake. She was hoping I would be released and come home. But the judge ruled against bail because it was a death penalty or life imprisonment case. Though I was dejected and solemn, I never thought about the death penalty, there was something greater in me that wouldn't allow it, but I also didn't have confidence in the judicial system.

I was returned to jail. While I was not able to speak directly with Grem that day, we acknowledged each other with warm smiles and head nods in the courtroom. After the hearing, Grem mouthed the words, *"I love you Fiqqi."* Later that afternoon, before returning back to the jail, a Deputy Sheriff came to my holding cell with a package. This was highly unusual, as no packages were allowed for prisoners. But when the judge had ruled against bail, Grem went to one of the Sheriffs and worked her verbal magic to allow me to have the cake. Despite the setback, I felt that God truly had a hand in my life.

The Commonwealth chose to retry my case. Two-and-half years later, my case was on the docket. On advice from Mr. Siegel, I opted for a bench trial. Mr. Siegel felt that the judge assigned to my trial, William Mazzola, a man small in stature with a full head of gray hair and glasses, was reportedly the type of judge who was not afraid to make difficult decisions.

On Monday, May 12, 2003, both attorneys presented their case to the judge. After his presentation, Mr. Siegel further emphasized that the prosecutors had not made their case and he said, "The defense rests." Closing arguments were heard by Judge William Mazzola. What seemed like an eternity to me, was actually an hour for the judge to read the arguments and then render his decision.

When the judge returned to the bench around 4:30 that afternoon, I was stone-faced. Judge Mazzola was wearing his glasses when he entered the courtroom, but he took them off and let the silence build before he said anything. The deafening silence lasted what seemed like 20 minutes to me, when in fact only several minutes had passed before the judge finally spoke. He looked out over the courtroom. The victim's family was present, and so was my mom, Rowdy, and Grem.

This was only the second time that I laid eyes on my mom and Rowdy. She didn't visit me during my time in jail. I specifically asked Shaunda to not bring Rowdy or my other children to the jail after seeing Rowdy's reaction the first and only time he visited me. When it was time to leave, he screamed repeatedly I want to go with my dad! The C.O.s had to pry him from me because he wouldn't let me go once the visit had ended, and now here he was about to hear whether I would be coming home or going to prison forever.

The judge said that what he was going to say would anger some people. He acknowledged the arguments by both attorneys and then said, "I find Rafiq Williams not guilty." He banged his gavel and walked out of the courtroom. I heard the words, sat down in my seat, put my head in my hands, and sobbed. It felt like a 500-pound weight had been lifted off my shoulders. My son ran over to me, began hugging me, and kept repeating, "My daddy is coming home! My daddy is coming home!" The Sheriff quickly intervened and returned my son to his seat.

I went with the sheriff to be returned to the jail where they would process my release. While the final stages of my release were being prepared, I was stunned to learn that because of old traffic court citations, for driving without a license, I owed the court about $1400. Because of these fines, my release was in jeopardy. For one of the first times since my arrest five years earlier, I felt despair. But something greater in me kept fighting internally. C.O. Sgt. Trueheart came up to me and told me that he was going to help take care of the traffic court warrant and see if he could get a subpoena issued to get me released that night.

I was present for the 6:15 head count at the jail. I was then issued a subpoena to appear in traffic court the following Monday, May 19, 2003. Finally, around 7 p.m., I was released from the jail. My dad was waiting for me in the visitor's lobby. When I saw my pop I gave him a big hug, he took my bags, and we headed to his car.

Meanwhile, on the other side of the city, Grem had left the court proceedings at 4:30 that afternoon and headed to the market. She had a celebration to prepare for me. There would be a houseful of guests, about 16, including my parents, my brother, cousins, and friends, who would be coming to celebrate my homecoming. In less than three hours, she prepared all of my favorite foods, none of which I had had in five long years: fried chicken, collard greens, macaroni and cheese, and my absolute favorite, Grem's special lemon cake.

We arrived at my mom's house for the celebration around 7:45. I kept looking around, constantly observing the neighborhood for any unwanted guests. I was on edge but at the same time, I was elated about being home. And then I saw him. Rowdy came running out to the car to greet me with tears of joy and relief streaming down his face. I didn't even realize that I was crying. I had never felt such raw emotion before, my wolf persona prevented me from allowing such feelings.

When I walked into my mom's house, I could smell the fried chicken still cooking. There were hugs all around along with smiles and laughter. We dined on Grem's cooking for several hours. I was finally home.

Later that night, me and Rowdy went to Shaunda's house to be with her and my two other children. Initially, it felt weird being in person with everyone after so many years of being away from my loved ones. My two other children were asleep and didn't know that I was home until the following morning. I felt like I was in a trance being back in the house with Shaunda and my children. While it was my fervent hope that I would be home one day, now that it was a reality, it didn't seem real. Shaunda and I talked and had loving, physical contact.

Unfortunately, a good night's sleep was difficult as I was plagued with a nightmare that I had been mistakenly released and had to be sent back to jail. In the morning when Arti, Nya, and Rowdy, were awake, another celebration of my homecoming awaited.

When Arti and Nya saw that I was home they did a double-take before realizing it was me. They ran over to me and jumped on me, hugging me tightly with tears streaming down their faces. They did not want to let go of me.

However, the joy of being home with Shaunda was short-lived as, unbeknownst to me, she had been spiraling out of control with her drug use. Before I went to jail, she just smoked weed. Now I observed more troubling behaviors, staying up all hours, missing money, and finding straws. This reminded me of living with my mom and finding empty cocaine bags around the house with these same straws.

I called my brother Miz to find out what had been going on with Shaunda while I was in jail. What I learned was that my mom had turned Shaunda into a drug addict. It angered me to find out my mom was responsible for turning Shaunda out. I had already hated my mom because of her drug use, and now I have to be subjected to this again. I made up my mind that I would not allow my children to grow up around this, but didn't know how I would remove them just yet.

True to my commitment to my freedom, the following Monday after my release from jail, I appeared in traffic court. The judge had been briefed about me. He looked up at me, now a 27-year-old man, and said, *"Consider yourself blessed today. Now go get yourself a driver's license!"* All of the tickets and costs were thrown out. Two weeks later, I secured a Driver's Ed book and studied it from cover to cover. I went to the Mayfair section of the city to take the computer test which I passed on the first try.

Two weeks following the computer test, I took the driving portion of the test at the Oxford Circle location. Typical of me doing whatever I had to do to survive, I drove myself to the testing location on my learner's permit because I had no other way to get there. Driving my father's burgundy Chevy Lumina, I parked the car near the testing center. Once there, opportunists were on the scene who would allow you to use their cars to take the test for a mere $75. After having driven illegally for more than 15 years, I was allowed to drive, legally. At 27, I finally had a driver's license.

For me, earning my driver's license brought me one step closer to legalizing my life and being a productive and law-abiding citizen. It felt good! This simple license reinforced my hope and desire that my life would now be different. The driver's license made me feel truly free.

I never got back into dealing drugs for the lifestyle or to be the biggest and richest dealer ever. I got back into it as a means of survival. One thing I have learned in life is it takes seconds to make a bad decision, but it can take years to rectify that bad decision.

Rafiq Williams

Chapter VII The Cartel

Though deep down I craved a life like I'd seen on TV, one with a family at the dinner table, a mom or dad making sure homework and chores were done, the fact was that after I was released from jail I couldn't get a job. I was 27 years old and had earned my GED during my five-year bid. I was willing to work anywhere, but KFC and 20 other businesses I applied to that were paying minimum wage would not hire me. This frustrated me. I'm trying to do right and live right, yet I can't find a job. I know what to do, but I am desperately trying to stay away from hustling again.

I eventually left Shaunda. A friend let me stay in his apartment in Germantown. Her drug use, which had started when I went to jail, had become unbearable. I had a conversation with my children before I moved out and explained how I was feeling. They said, *"It's cool Dad if you move out; we know you love us. We want you to be happy. Are you going to come back and get us?"* I said, *"Absolutely."* She eventually violated her probation and was jailed.

When she was jailed my children, who were 8, 9, and 12, came to live with me in a home at 23rd and Ontario that I purchased at a sheriff's sale for tax liens and fully remodeled about a year after I got out. I wanted to give them a life where we have family dinners, I check their homework and they do chores. After six months of job hunting, I realized my dream was not aligned with my reality. That's it. It was time to get busy.

I started hustling again. And again, I was good at it. Most importantly, it provided for my family. I was determined to make a different life for my children. Hustling seemed like the only option I had until I figured out something else. I had ideas, but I realized I had no clue how to get where I wanted to go: a business entrepreneur, a lawyer, or go to school to get my degree. I knew I was smart and would work twice as hard as anyone else, but I couldn't even get my foot in the door for a fast-food job selling chicken. Back in school, they showed us jobs like lawyers, but that's the endpoint. They didn't teach us how to get there. I thought: Just show me the way, and I'll get there! All I knew was the world of the streets. It came down to survival: I have a family, and we gotta eat.

Gone was the champagne-colored Lexus ES 300 of my younger days. This time, I kept a low profile. I drove a slightly beat-up Chevy minivan and kept my circle tight. I had two trusted friends who hustled for me, and who obeyed my rule that Sundays were off-limits for drug business. I was living an irony, one foot in each world: a church-going Christian and a gun-carrying drug dealer. I was both.

Every day I struggled to reconcile the deep belief in God that I'd developed in jail with the way I earned my living. But come Sunday, it was God's day and Williams family time. After church, I took my children, and often Miz's two children, to eat at Old Country Buffet on Roosevelt Boulevard in Feltonville. Sometimes we would go play games at Dave & Buster's afterward. I had money now, and God help the unknowing soul who violated my Sunday family time to try and do a deal. They were dealt with by the side of me nobody wanted to deal with more than once.

When we got home on Sundays, I made sure my two sons and daughter were packed up, showered, and ready for the start of the school week. Their clothes were cleaned, their lunches packed, and they slept in tidy bedrooms because I demanded it. I ran a tight ship, and sometimes too tight I know now.

The way I earned my living during those years still bothers me at times, 20-something years down the road, but I was determined that no child of mine would be neglected. I was taking a risk every day to provide for them and to ensure that we survived. While my friends were out partying like 20-somethings, I was raising a family. Truth is, I wanted a family life. I craved a family life. Now I had the opportunity to provide a family life. I remember staying awake some nights in jail praying for the opportunity to be with my children again and enjoy the simple things in life.

I never got back in the game for the lifestyle. I got back into it because one day my son Rowdy came to me and asked me for a dollar, and I didn't have one to give him. He then asked me for 50 cents, and I didn't have it. My son went down to asking for 25 cents from me, and I didn't have it. Then he patted my back and said, *"It's ok, Dad. I know you'd give it to me if you had it."* The pain and the shame of that encounter cut deep, and at that moment I was determined to figure something out. A father is supposed to provide for his children, and in that moment, I felt like less of a man. We couldn't have this type of encounter again. It was time to do something.

I did not want to continue the cycle I'd known. Deep down, I knew there was a better life out there, and I was going to find a way to get it. My whole life I knew only one male who had a real job, my Uncle Tone, who lived in New Jersey. He tried to set an example for us, and he could never understand why we didn't follow in his footsteps. He wanted desperately to break the generational cycle that ravaged our family, mainly the men. Except for him, everybody else I knew hustled for a living. Until I figured out how to survive without living this way, I had to hustle. I had to get back in the game. It was survival.

The money came quickly. My family was stable. My children had everything they needed and more. But so many others in the neighborhood and my extended family did not. In my dilemma of living with one foot in each world, I was always generous with the money I made. I used a big portion of my income to establish a local basketball team, the North Philly Aztecs. I was the coach.

The team was talented, but many families could not afford things like pricey basketball sneakers. With my drug money, I bought the whole team uniforms, and sneakers for some. These boys were staying off the streets, training after school, being mentored, and we were winning. Our team clinched two Recreation League championships in Philly, in 2007 and 2008.

However, my players could not afford to enter the more competitive tournaments to continue their winning, and I couldn't live with that. I wanted my boys to get out of the hood and see some of the world. I wanted to give them the chance to run against some of the best young teams in the country. I spent $4,000 of drug money to cover the entry fees, transportation, and hotel costs for the Aztec's road trip to Cleveland, Ohio so we could play in the LeBron James Shooting Stars Tournament. This tournament featured some of the country's best up-and-coming young talent, so it was a good measuring stick for my players. It was a great opportunity for the team. We were underdogs, but I knew it was a good life experience. Many of my players were used to being labeled amongst the best in Philly, but not here. They would have to prove themselves.

They showed me. My scrappy Aztecs won game after game and eventually won the bronze medal game in a pool of 100 or so teams. I was thrilled that I had given the boys an opportunity to prove something to themselves beyond the boundaries of the neighborhood. Soon, though, my boundaries were expanded beyond the neighborhood as well, but in ways that became the worst days of my life.

Part of my desire to build a different life for my children was to meet a woman with the same family-oriented goals. One weekend I flew to Atlanta to attend a popular hair show. I knew plenty of women would be there, showing off the latest in cuts, colors, wigs, and weaves. Many of them, I hoped, were Christian women who shared my beliefs and desire for a better life.

A romance wasn't sparked, but my drug business exploded and got much more dangerous after this weekend in Atlanta; I'm talking a different level of danger than what a corner boy with a gun tucked in the waistband of his baggy jeans would experience. A strange encounter in Atlanta moved me into the big leagues of the game - the biggest. I began hustling for an international drug cartel.

In the game, people recognize one of their kind, and although I was trying to keep a low profile, something about the way I carried myself made a slick, Spanish-speaking man quietly approach me at the hair show. *"Eh, ¿Juegas el juego?"* I understood, but pretended that I didn't. The man had asked me if I, *"played the game." I* said, *"No comprende."* The man switched to English. *"Do you get busy?"*

I could tell the guy knew the life because he was using language that could not be held against him if I was an undercover agent, but language that was common among hustlers. Handing me a piece of paper, the man said, *"I know my people. Give me a call. I promise it will be worth your while."* Later that night I called, and we met at a restaurant. Over a dinner of lobsters, shrimp, and steak, I made a deal with the devil. Almost instantly I regretted it, but the money was unbelievable. The only reason I even considered dealing with this guy in the first place was because my connect back in Philly was recently indicted, and I was looking for a new line. I could continue to guarantee my children a good life and I to help others. Once I agreed, I knew I could fulfill my obligation because I always delivered.

Within a week my international connect was organizing the transport of a car to Philly packed with kilos of coke. I had seen a lot of drugs in my life, my mom was a cokehead, my pop became a heroin addict, and plenty of people hustled in my neighborhood. My neighborhood was the place where White men and women in expensive cars came to buy. Through the years I dabbled in drugs, too, nothing hard, but thanks be to God, I never got dependent. The cartel operation I was now a part of ran more coke than I could have dreamed of; and the money, over almost two decades ago, was three times the salary I made when I was a school principal.

The cartel gave me a trial run, with a date to return the money for the work. Days before the deadline I sold my 25 keys and handed over $412,500, earning me instant respect. My reward was to sell 75 keys of coke worth $1,237,500. Again and again, I flipped my stuff quicker than expected. This went on for two years.

I came up with a savvy plan: most of the work on the streets was stepped on, meaning it was not pure, but cut with baking soda or any white powder. I sold my stuff pure. I always had customers.

I kept working with the cartel until the global recession hit in 2008. I was still rolling in cash, but I felt tormented. We were doing well now. My family was ok. I couldn't tell anyone, but I wanted out. However, in this game nobody gets out. I knew I'd have to find a way. I couldn't live with myself anymore.

I continued coaching, making dinner, checking homework, going to church, and selling huge quantities of coke. I always said I was willing to do anything to give my children a better life, but not this. For the first time in my life, I was in over my head. I was operating in a violent, secretive, and complicated world that I'd seen glimpses of in movies. This was real. I was living a life where people disappeared, where a small infraction or a whiff of betrayal could mean a bullet to the head.

For the first time in my life, I was scared, and I was not scared easily. When I was eight years old, my house was robbed one night and one of the robbers pointed a gun at me. I knew with the cartel I was in deeper than I ever wanted to be, I knew the consequences of trying to leave, but still I had to find a way out.

I was a man now but I'd grown up with violence, and even in prison I did not feel scared. I knew I could hold my own. With the cartel, I was in a savage league. Not only was I unsure I could hold my own, I didn't want to. I didn't want that life.

I had a relationship with God now and wondered how I had gotten here. I wanted to be a good son to him. I wanted to be a good father. I honored Sundays, but that wasn't enough for me. The dichotomy of having one foot in two different worlds, magnified now by the level I was operating on, troubled my heart. I had spent six months in the hole, 23 hours a day in a cell so narrow I could touch the sidewalls with my arms stretched out.

That isolation, the first place I lived without violence, is where I found God. Believe it or not, it turned out to be a blessing to me, even though I was there for a violent act committed within the jail. That's God, I learned. He knew me, my life, my adaptations, and he knew I wanted better. In his infinite wisdom, he knew he had to get me alone, away from all distractions.

In the hole, I had read the Bible and was amazed at God's promises. Hours of prayer and reading in my cell allowed me to gain an intimate understanding of God's extraordinary personal love for me and for every person. I had promised God I would make something good of my life if I got out. When I started working for the cartel, I did not forget that I was not keeping my promise.

As the recession of 2008 dragged on shipment after shipment of drugs got seized at the ports, causing my line to stop trying to send work for a while. My mind began to race about getting out. Could this be my opportunity to leave the game? How would I do it? All these thoughts were running through my head, but one thing was for sure: this was my opportunity.

The best thing that happened to me was that recession. The United States had launched a major war on drugs, nationally and internationally. Ports where our drugs were smuggled began to close, first for a week, then two, then three, as shipments were discovered. I learned the basics of economics: supply and demand. My supply dried up, but the demand remained. Droughts usually led to warfare on the streets and an increase in drug-related robberies or home invasions. Inflation even takes place in the drug game. Those who were left with work during droughts would usually double the price.

My position was unique. Working with the cartel, I was an operative on both battlefields, supply and demand. I saw in it a sliver of hope to get out alive. It would be a huge risk, but it was the only chance I had. My kids were worth the risk of me getting back into the game, and they were certainly worth the risk of getting out.

Since day one in Atlanta, I used an alias with the cartel. I knew the game. I knew to reveal nothing, not the smallest detail about my personal life. No one knew my real name. No one knew where I lived. Most importantly, I used a new burner phone every day so I couldn't be tracked. With the daily burner, I called a cartel connection and then followed orders. Often, but not always, I picked up the drugs in hidden garages in Philly. Usually, but not always, I took the cartel's proceeds to Pittsburgh, five hours west.

I was closed-mouthed, operated almost invisibly, and kept growing the business. They kept giving me more and more and it kept my family solid. I always paid the cartel before the money was due. I earned the trust and respect of the cartel, but I was losing respect for myself. I had put my family at great risk, though I had gotten back in the game to protect them.

By the time shipments repeatedly began to stall, I had paid my debts, as usual. As I waited for a new shipment to get through and the delays continued, I decided it was now or never. I was getting out. I stopped buying burner phones. The cartel had no way to contact me. They didn't know my name or where I lived, and I had done right by them. To me, it was over. Or so I thought.

One afternoon, about a month later, I took my two dogs for a walk. My dogs were an illegal breed called Presa Canario. They are like pit bulls on steroids. We were walking on a little back street in my North Philly neighborhood when several men from the cartel grabbed me and told me I was coming with them in a van they had there, running. It was a Saturday afternoon in spring, and my son was playing basketball on the back block near our street. *"Rowdy, come get the dogs,"* I hollered. I told him I had to run out for a little while.

As I climbed in behind the tinted windows of the van, I knew my destiny. These guys don't play. I thought for sure that was the last day I'd see my kids. Please, God, no, I silently prayed. This can't be the end. Inside the dark van, one man spoke: *"My uncle wants to see you."* I knew what that meant, and it was not good news. Uncle rarely came to the United States, but he had come for me because I was a major earner who had gone silent.

The four men and I took the elevator to a top-floor suite of an upscale hotel in Philly where Uncle was standing to greet me. I didn't know if they'd kill me here, but I knew they would kill me to send a message to others. I'd met Uncle before, but not on American soil. His thick black hair curled out of his cowboy hat. On his feet were the finest two-tone snakeskin cowboy boots. On his fingers shimmered many gold rings. Mouth closed, he smiled at me. *"My friend, you don't call,"* he said calmly. *"We don't talk. You hurt my feelings, my friend."*

I knew this could be the end for me, but I had always been quick on my feet, thinking fast to escape danger. I showed proper respect to Uncle by first telling him I was not working for anyone else. That was the most important thing for him. *"I know that, my friend. That is the reason you're still alive. But you leave me this way?"* He gestured for me to sit.

In that conversation, I broke the cardinal rule. I got personal about my life. It poured out of me. I told Uncle I was raising three children alone. I told him how much I loved them and wanted to give them a better life. I told him about the North Philly Aztecs, about the good grades my children were getting in school, and how much I enjoyed doing things with them. I had made a stable home. Selling drugs had helped me do that, but I just couldn't take the risk anymore. I was all they had. Years before while in jail, I told Uncle, I had promised God that I would do something good with my life if I got out, and I needed to keep that promise.

"I know what you've been doing," Uncle said quietly. *"I would like to spend more time with my family."* He didn't let me off easy. He allowed the threat of death to loom in the room during the conversation. But he let me go. He warned me that if I ever got back in the game: *"You call me. Or else, my friend, you and I know how this ends."*

He ordered his men to take me back to my home. They were as stunned as I was. On the silent ride back one man finally spoke: *"He's never let anyone walk away."* I silently thanked God for his protection and blessing. I was out, and this time I planned to stay out.

As a Christian, God calls on us to be obedient to his word. Disobedience comes in many forms, just like many of us would discipline our children for being disobedient. We should expect discipline from God for being disobedient as well.

Rafiq Williams

Chapter VIII Disobedience

I beat a death sentence for the second time. Walking away from an international cartel as one of the highest earners in the United States was an unparalleled feat.

I knew I was smart and fiercely ambitious. I felt a new hope for my life. On the surreal ride home from the hotel meeting with Uncle a thought crystallized in my brain: I have an open road. My true dream was never to be a prince in a cartel or king of a North Philly drug corner, but king of a castle with my children and a wife. But how? The only clues I had about that lifestyle were from watching TV. That wasn't real.

To get a new start, I relied on my past and my instincts. Both were grounded for so many years in day-to-day survival: Somewhere to sleep, something to eat, someplace to shower. Most importantly, at all times I needed to prove myself on the street. No more. My road was open. I could now be a normal guy, enjoying the simple things in life. Unfortunately, I did not know how to make the one life I wanted from the two parts I now had: the same demoralizing environment and my newfound faith.

I denied the voice whispering to me to take time and align my decisions with God's path. I overpowered that soft voice with a louder one in my head. I'd been spared death many times as I grew up. The fact that I walked around alive, a free man, I now believed there was a greater plan for my future. Then I went and disobeyed every red flag thrown my way.

The trouble was I had enormous amounts of cash, but had never held a job. I wanted to invest in real estate but had no credit established. I had to figure something out. No sense in having money if you can't do anything with it.

While I was shopping at Neiman Marcus at the King of Prussia Mall, I met an attractive and lively woman who identified as Muslim. I soon learned she had excellent credit. My heart whispered caution to me, but I disregarded it. All these years I followed my instincts, and now here I was disregarding them. I came up with a master plan, or so I thought. If I married her, I'd put one foot on the open road of my new life. I did what I knew. I played the cards I was dealt, and I kept moving.

Against my family's wishes, nine months later I married the girl from the store. Together we began to buy houses in Philly. I could have paid cash and bought an entire city block, but paying cash would have been far too risky so I focused on building credit with my wife.

Though my relationship with my teenage children had begun to fray, my eldest son Arti one day reminded me of the solid, though unusual, foundation I had laid with them. Arti handed me a plastic drawstring shopping bag filled with $80,000. I had forgotten I'd told him to hold it as I was heading out to do a deal late one night. Six months later he reminded me that he had the bag, and not one dollar was missing. I thought instantly that I never have to worry about this one stealing from me. I felt blessed to be the father of such an honest child.

However, my relationship deteriorated with Arti, Rowdy, and Nya. I was a taskmaster. My crib had rules, and a new one was that I insisted the children respect my wife. If they didn't like my rules, I told them they could leave. And one by one, they did.

My arrogance in doing things my way, because I usually got the result I wanted, caused a rift with the most important people in my life. First, Arti left. At 15, he ran away and ended up living with his maternal grandmother. He returned a year later. Then, Nya ran away at age 12. She returned for some years but she continued to clash with my wife. At 17, Nya had enough, feeling that I bowed to my wife and never defended her. She left again, this time for good. My thought at that time was that my children were rebelling because they had never had a stable mother figure. I reasoned that they weren't accustomed to a two-parent home. They'd never had to share me.

I wouldn't hear them when they told me my wife was a party girl and a cheater. I told them to stop lying and stay in a child's place. I felt that a husband should stand by his wife, as the Bible taught. I had never been a husband before, and I realize now that I knew so little about healthy relationships. I was doing what I'd seen on TV.

The last child to go, the one who said he'd never leave me, was Rowdy. He didn't like how my wife pointed out everything that he did wrong and acted as if she was better than his mother. When Rowdy walked out of the house with nothing but basketball shorts and Nike slides on his feet, it changed everything for me. I showed no emotions, but it cut me deep. My children were the only people in life that I always felt belonged to me and would never betray me. After all, I took countless risks to provide them with an opportunity to have a better life.

To ease my pain, I put them in the category of others who hurt me throughout my life. It was easier to deal with it that way. The hurt from that time made me realize that though I thought my intentions were good, I had disobeyed God. He'd thrown me plenty of warning flags. I'd veered off the new open road I was given after jail, after walking away from Uncle. In my heartbreak I learned that disobedience comes in many forms, but none worse than spiritual disobedience. Here I was trying to provide a better life for my children, but unknowingly brought destruction and division to my family. Pride and arrogance will cause the best of us to fall.

My spiritual beliefs took a backseat to my ambition when I chose to marry for the wrong reasons, and steadily the consequences began to mount: my children left. That was the worst. Then, my house was robbed when we weren't home and I began obsessively staying up nights to keep watch and protect my wife. At about the same time, I developed a life-threatening auto-immune disease that took years to properly diagnose and treat. The disease, Sarcoidosis, caused searing lesions to erupt all over my skin, and the medication I was prescribed almost shut my liver down. It was a tough time, one of the worst.

On top of that, my pop died, unexpectedly. I remember sitting in my bedroom preparing to get in the shower after a long day working in the yard to install a vinyl fence to secure my dogs. My dad had helped me the day before with some of the fencing but called that morning to tell me he would be going to New Jersey to help his brother, my Uncle Tone, renovate his bathroom. I said cool; I'll see you tomorrow.

Little did I know there would be no tomorrow for us. I got a call at 8:15 that night from my Cousin Bern. She screamed, *"Fiq, Uncle Mike gone Fiq!"* I said, *"What? Bern don't play with me. What are you talking about?"* She said call Uncle Tone. They rushed your father to the hospital, and Uncle Tone won't tell us anything. He said, *"He just told me to call you and tell the family to get here right away."*

I threw my cell phone across the room in anger. I paced around the room before gathering myself and tried calling my Uncle Tone. He answered the phone and said, *"They are in the back working on your dad, just get your mom and get here now Rafiq!"* I jumped in the car and drove straight to my mom's house and told her, *"Get in the car. Now! Something is wrong with dad and Uncle Tone isn't saying much."* My mom instantly burst into tears and said, *"Ra your dad is gone, I can feel it! I got a weird feeling about 30 minutes ago but didn't know what it was about."* She then collapsed, but before she could hit the ground, I caught her. I guided her into the car and sped off. It was a two-hour drive, but I made it to the hospital in an hour and 15 minutes. My mom cried the whole ride.

Many thoughts raced through my head, but I kept hoping for the best. Once we arrived at the hospital my uncle took my mom and me into an area to wait for the rest of the family. My brother Miz was back in prison so I knew that whatever the outcome of this night would be, I would be handling it by myself.

I began to get impatient waiting for the others to arrive. A few times my uncle caught a side of me that many wished they'd never see. Finally, Grem arrived. I sent for the doctor, who began to give a dissertation about my dad's condition, when I interrupted him. *"Man, just tell me whether my pop is alive!"* At that, the doctor said, *"Unfortunately…"* He couldn't even get out the rest of his sentence before my mom, Grem, and Bern let out uncontrollable sobs between screams.

After consoling my mom and Grem, I told the doctor that I needed to see my dad. Everything my dad had ever done at that moment didn't matter to me. I laid my head by his side. It was the first time I can remember crying in a long time. The irony was that the person who told me crying meant I was soft, now had me in tears because of his death. This marked one of the most painful experiences in my life.

My children running away was the second most painful experience of my life. The stubborn spirit that had served me my whole life, that cloak of the wolf I wore to stay alive, began to soften. Finally, in my suffering, I yielded to the whisper that had been tapping at my heart for years. I got closer to God more than I ever had, and then the revelation came. All the destruction and devastation in my life was a direct result of disobedience. I married someone who did not spiritually align with me. I used my free will and chose to marry anyway for the world I wanted to create. That world was now shattered.

Many nights my wife snuck home at daybreak, and I finally told her that I had enough. I finally saw what others had been seeing. I never counted the cost of what the consequences would be for my disobedience. Now, I doubled down on asking God for forgiveness and tried following his plan for my life. As a hard-headed man I'd made many mistakes, but I usually don't make them twice.

Society teaches us that love is connected to our feelings. The problem with that is feelings are temporary. I have learned that real love loves despite not feeling it. Real love never gives up, never loses faith, is always hopeful, and endures through every circumstance.

Rafiq Williams
1 Corinthians 13:7

Chapter IX Real Love

Two years later they were all there, clapping and hollering for me as I crossed the stage with a degree in my hand. Things were not perfect, but they were better once I decided to let God lead me.

One person who was not there was my wife. My marriage had disintegrated. I renewed a relationship with my kids and graduated from the Community College of Philadelphia with an Associate Degree in Criminal Justice. My children had insisted on coming, and it meant the world to me. My mom and Miz were present for my graduation as well. My mom told me she was proud of me, something I rarely heard from either of my parents. After the ceremony, we all went out to eat at Buffalo Wild Wings. I looked around the table and felt the love that day. This truly was one of the happiest days of my life.

Though my adult children appreciate me now for my steady hand in their lives, we've all come to realize that my traumatic upbringing affected my parenting. I was hard. That's all I knew. I didn't want them to experience some of the pitfalls and traumas I experienced growing up. When they fell I ordered them to get up. When they cried, I told them to stop being a baby.

I realized that my inability to show or express emotion prevented me from allowing them to be emotional, even at times when it was warranted. I just did not know how to be soft with them. Thankfully, they say they always knew I loved them. There are things they remember now, that showed them I loved them, even though I didn't praise them enough, hug enough, or listen enough.

Nya remembers me at the stove, determined to learn how to cook. When I got custody of my children, Grem said she couldn't have her great-grandchildren eating Oodles of Noodles every night. She shared some of her secret recipes, showed me which pots or pans to use, and how high to keep the fire. I wanted home-cooked meals for my family, not fast food. We sat and ate a hot meal every night. I enjoyed that time together. That was me loving them.

More challenging than learning how to cook dinner, was learning how to braid Nya's hair when she was in elementary school. I didn't do anything too fancy. I appreciated the compliments I got from the mothers for my attempts. I couldn't have my baby girl going to school looking any kind of way, and risk being teased by other children. That was me loving her, the best way I knew how.

Education was a big deal in my home. I often assigned extra homework and made every activity into a learning experience. Etched in my brain is what my mom constantly told us: *"People can take a lot of things from you, but they can't take your education."* I made it my mission to make sure my children were constantly being educated. They hated my stance on education, but it was my one non-negotiable while raising them. I remember withholding their Christmas gifts one year from them due to bad report cards. Needless to say, they didn't get bad report cards again. That, too, was me trying to love them.

One summer, I wanted to teach them business concepts so I bought a deep freezer and filled it with water ice. It sat on our front porch and served as a makeshift water ice stand. I turned it into a daily business, and they earned a weekly check. They had to tally the sales for the week, subtract their expenses, and find out how much profit we made. Then they'd argue over who got how much of the profits, because one had good ideas, one worked harder, and one ate more water ice than he sold. I would laugh at them when they had these spats. I left it to them to sort out, but I loved seeing them thinking, and having difficult conversations with one another. After they had reached a consensus on who should get what, I explained to them how difficult it is to go into business with partners. They thought I was hard, but I thought I was loving them.

Day trips and vacations were a priority and always included something new to learn, a unique experience, something to read, or a map to look over. My son Arti jokes that I was "active" in their schooling while making it clear that he is making a huge understatement. He says I knew the name of every teacher in their school, and they knew mine. We laugh about it now as we look back. He would say, *"Dad you were drawing back then!"* [15] A father himself now, Arti says that though it was often annoying, it made him know that I cared, and for that I am grateful.

In the summer I ran the Williams Family Summer School. Each day my children picked a word from the dictionary, spelled it, and gave me the definition. They also read daily and answered comprehension questions from me I would read a few specific chapters and ask questions from those chapters. This kept them accountable to read the whole book because they never knew what chapters I would read, and question them on. Don't get me wrong, they played plenty. They had Play Stations, Xboxes and my baby girl played her Wii.

Today, Nya practices a similar routine with her fourth grader, my granddaughter, Safiya. She is more affectionate, and gentle than I was, but she models her school approach after mine.

My focus as a father was a far cry from what I'd known as a child. When I was 15 and had a baby on the way, I just stopped going to school. The way I saw it, every hour I spent in school was an hour I was losing money, an hour some other guy was making money I could have had

---

[15] Drawing back then—making a scene

in my pocket. No one, not my mom, not my pop, no aunt or uncle, no school officials, ever told me to stay in school.

Truth be told, my mom didn't know that I dropped out of school because I was living on my own. I was hardheaded and probably wouldn't have listened, but I wonder why no one ever tried, slapped me upside the head and told me to stay in school. No one laid down the law and told me to stay out of the street life.

No one looked out for me, for my future. That is the reason I was hard on my kids, but they sure knew someone was looking out for them, that someone wanted them to have a future.

Though I had started my college journey, and would never turn back, lessons from my past were valuable as I began a more challenging academic path. I wanted to earn my bachelor's degree. I needed paper[16] to accomplish this. Even though I was making dough with the cartel, I had a hustler's mentality and had started a side business providing security. Once I left the cartel, I realized that could be my source of income and I could continue my schooling.

My security company protected Philly nightclubs. I knew I wanted out of the drug business altogether, but I had no qualifications to be hired for anything. What I did

---

[16] Paper—money

have was a fierce presence, a prison-hard body, a good mind, and hustle. I applied for a special license from the Pennsylvania State Police to start the security business to carry firearms while performing security work.

On the surface, it seems astonishing that I would be granted permission to carry concealed weapons, but legally I had been found not guilty of the two charges that had sent me to jail, so I received the license.

From 2008-2011 I strapped one gun into a leg holster and one around my waist and went to work. My company grew, and in a wry twist, remembered how I employed two state troopers who stopped me one night. This was while I was on a cartel drug run from Pittsburgh to Philly, during my time when I was still with them. At 2 a.m., careful to be driving the speed limit, I was stopped on a highway by two White troopers. I knew the drill a Black man needed to follow. I spoke respectfully to the troopers and stayed cool. That was not easy because I was carrying 150 kilos of cocaine worth 2.5 million dollars in my Chevy Minivan.

If things went sideways, I was doomed. I answered their questions as to why I was driving so late and why I was driving fast by telling them I was coming from a security expo in Pittsburgh, even though I wasn't driving above the 50-mph speed limit. I handed one of them my company business card. As the troopers shined their flashlights in the back of the van, they saw boxes upon boxes. Security equipment, I told them. One slip-up and I would be doing at least 20 years in state prison, or worse at a federal penitentiary.

One of the benefits of learning to shut my emotions off early in life was that I kept my cool. In addition to the expo, I told the troopers, I had also just finished a security job in Pittsburgh. At one point I even asked one of the troopers if he wanted to see some of the cool stuff companies wanted me to try out. Man, what was I thinking? Those boxes held bricks of cocaine.

The troopers had perked up when they heard the word security and inferred that they liked to pick up extra money moonlighting as security guards. They asked me if I had any work for them. I told them that I had some work for them and if they gave me a call in the morning, I'd let them know what I had available. With that, I eased my way back onto the road, with no ticket.

As I drove off, I thought, heck yeah, I would like to have guys like that to work for my company. As always, I delivered. I hired both troopers for the next two years and paid them each $150 for a five-hour shift to patrol a nightclub parking lot in Philly.

A few hours after the stop I delivered the cocaine to the cartel garage, drove home, and made breakfast for my kids. They ate with no idea how close they came to being without their father for the foreseeable future.

I was still trying to find my way to the normalcy I craved and I stayed focused on my kids. One evening Arti had 10th grade math homework that involved exponents. He asked me for help and I found I was finally tapped out, unable to help him. I despised that feeling. I was telling my son to do his homework, but I didn't even know how to do it. I felt like a hypocrite. I admitted to him that I did not know how to solve the problems. He gave me a quizzical look because according to him, he never heard me sound defeated before. I gave Arti a pep talk, about not giving up, turning in the homework even if it was wrong, and paying attention in class.

The next day I bought a book called, "Math for Dummies." By the time Arti came home, I was ready to help with his homework. That was the way I knew how to show love: I had learned exponents in a matter of hours. With a smile, Arti remembered that experience and said, *"I have never seen you fail at anything. Anything."* That was by the grace of God.

Another step on my journey of leaving the street life and finding a way forward was when my son Rowdy showed promise as a high school football player. There were murmurs that he might be able to play on the college level. I was on him day and night to keep his grades up. He could be the first in the family to go to college. This encouraged me as a father that I must be doing something right. As time passed and I pushed him about going to college, he came at me with a challenge of his own: *"I will, if you will."*

I'm a competitor. I accepted the challenge. After getting my GED, scoring among the best, and being encouraged by my teacher to pursue college, I got the ball rolling. Weeks later I sat at the kitchen table with books and papers around me. *"What are you doing, Dad?"* Rowdy asked. I said: *"I started college."* He smiled and said, *"Stop playing Dad!"* I pulled out my college I.D. and showed it to him. He said, *"Oh you ain't playing! You should've waited for me, so we could graduate together."*

I rose up and impressed my children and it made me feel good. I didn't have much experience with college, but I figured out the way forward and showed them the way. Education was our way forward. I realized it would unlock the doors closed to us, otherwise. If I wanted to be a drug dealer forever, then no, education wasn't needed, but I wanted something different, and this was the way.

My son Rowdy says that I conveyed somehow that I'd probably never see him graduate from high school. His memory is that I thought he'd most likely be dead or in prison because he was too much like me. I didn't fear anything, and neither did he.

All my children graduated high school. Rowdy and I attended college together for a few semesters while I was earning my Bachelor's Degree at Chestnut Hill College. It was surreal to attend college with him. I can't forget the many times he tried to cheat off my work, but the experience was a true blessing. Rowdy had gone to Cheyney University out of high school but had transferred so we could be together.

The first time we had class together was Intro to Drama. The teacher was taking attendance and got to my name and said, *"Oh this must be a mistake, they put down Rafiq Williams twice."* I laughed and said, *"It's not a mistake, that dude back there is my son."* The teacher was shocked, and said, *"This is the first time I had a father and son in the same class, are you sure you're not jerking my chain?"* I said, *"Trust me, he's my son, and I can't seem to get rid of him."* At that response, the whole class erupted in laughter.

Each one of my children gravitated to the field of education. My sons are teaching assistants at the school where I was the principal, and my daughter is working on her degree in Early Childhood Education. I was the first in my immediate family to graduate from college.

At 35-years old I landed a job as a classroom assistant in a school for at-risk students. I knew my path now. I knew those kids because I had been one of them, and I quickly thrived. At night, I continued college classes. During that time, I realized I wanted to advance to decision-making positions. That meant a position in leadership, so I continued to earn a Master's degree in Educational Leadership and passed the praxis to earn my school principal's certification through my alma mater Chestnut Hill College. As I climbed the ranks to become principal, I gave job opportunities to a fistful of other competent young men who grew up with my two boys.

    As a principal they said I strolled the corridors of the school day-to-day and exuded warmth and authority. I hope so. Sometimes they said I reminded them of Joe Clark, the principal from the acclaimed movie *Lean on Me*. Only I don't talk on a bullhorn. I made it a point to be visible, to know names, to bend down and help pull a hoodie over the head of a student running late, and then tell them to get to class. I kept deodorant in my desk drawer for students who needed it, and some came for it every morning.

    I could have never predicted that this would be my life now. Mr. Romanelli would be proud of me, having been a principal and now moving into a position as Dean of Students at one of the largest public high schools in Delaware. At these students' ages, I had no path other than the streets except the one I made, a surprise even to myself.

I get so much satisfaction from helping others know that they can find their way, too.

My greatest accomplishment of all was meeting the love of my life. I met her during my first week working at the school for at-risk students where I later became principal. She was a teaching assistant in a different classroom. I credit that woman, who is now my wife, Shay, with teaching me about real love, how to give it, and, much tougher, how to receive it.

For a couple of years, we were really good friends before becoming romantically involved. Shay came from a solid, loving home. We never would have crossed paths had it not been for the school. There was an instant connection. It was easy to laugh and joke with one another, but I still did not know how to love. She sensed it and nicknamed me "North Philly" for the hard edge I still carried. That nickname was like a badge of honor, as most from North Philly are known to be hard. Little did I know, that nickname would become a problem for us.

As time passed Shay got fed up with my inability to communicate from the heart and left me. One specific incident brought it all to a head for her. We had a conversation about no response to a text is a response. Stupid, right? In fact, stupid was the word that drove her over the edge. I told her if she believed that no response to a text is a response then she is stupid. We had never gotten into any arguments prior, nor had I ever called her a disrespectful name. It felt wrong the moment I said it, but being who I was then, I was like: It is what it is.

While downstairs making breakfast before heading to work, I kept having this nagging feeling to apologize so, shockingly, I did. I told her that I apologized for calling her stupid. She accepted my apology, but I could tell that the damage had been done. I had never learned how to be soft, affectionate, or emotional. I had molded myself to be exactly the opposite to survive. Gentleness, affection, and emotion were qualities of weakness in my world.

When she walked away, Shay was heartbroken, and surprisingly I was too. As a result, though the weirdest thing happened. When it comes to a relationship ending, whether it be family or otherwise, I respond with: It is what it is, and I move on.

This was different, I reached out to God. I knew I wanted to marry her, but she held firm that I needed to work on myself before she would consider marrying me. She was the first to recognize that I had unhealed trauma, though I hadn't shared much of my history with her. I had never viewed myself as someone who had been traumatized. That word wasn't a part of my vocabulary. She was adamant that unless I healed my wounds, she was not interested in us moving ahead.

I got to work spiritually, scrambling to find Christian mentors and to get even closer to God. Eight months had passed since Shay had left me. I realized I had found an ease in life, inner peace, and joy in a new way of living. With the help of God, I saw myself for the first time, and piece by piece dismantled the hard shell I had grown. It was grueling, but I wanted Shay back, as well as true peace and happiness.

I also found moments to apologize to my children and explain that there were reasons I behaved the way I did. I told them I now know I was too hard on them. I mentioned holding them back from expressing themselves emotionally. I was able to finally share with them my experience of being sexually abused by my cousin. They couldn't imagine something like that happening to me. That's because they constantly saw the strong and protective version of me. I told them this was why I struggled my whole life showing any form of emotion. They couldn't believe what they were hearing, I never was this open with anyone, but I knew they deserved to know. They opened their hearts and forgave me.

Over time I began to show Shay that I had learned how to be a real man, not the real man my upbringing had instilled in me. Through tears, I shared with her my trauma of being sexually abused. There were many things she didn't know about me. I was finally letting her in.

I was fearful she would look at me differently, but she didn't. That fear had kept me paralyzed for years, making sure people only saw me one way. Hard. Shay told me she knew I had a heart of gold buried inside, but knew she could not change me, only God could change me.

She reminded me of one instance in particular that clearly illustrated the change beginning in me. I thought it would have been when I opened up and shared my trauma with her, but it wasn't.

Where we live the scenery is beautiful; however, before she left me, I couldn't even see it. There are green fields, trees blowing in the wind, birds chirping outside our windows, and a quietness where she had found peace, but I had not. We started talking again by phone as friends, and I called her one day and said, *"I can finally see it! I see the beauty in the trees, fields, grass, and everything. I feel like I can breathe."*

I marked that day on my calendar. I knew in my bones, in my heart, that I was different. I felt a different kind of strength than I'd always relied upon. I was done being the wolf, being the man others feared to cross. That was false strength.

In Shay, I experienced a person who lived her faith and bubbled over with love. I wanted that, too. Though I had loved her and my children the only way I knew, it was not enough. It was incomplete. With Shay, I felt complete.

Learning how to love has been a journey, and I'm still learning, but Shay showed me the way. She showed me real love.

Rebirth doesn't mean to re-enter our mother's wombs and be born a second time. Rebirth is the transformation of one's mind, healing from past traumatic experiences, and overcoming past fears that keep you bound. It's a process!

Rafiq Williams

Chapter X Rebirth

Knowing what I wanted, and finding a way to achieve it, was a way of life for me. Some of my methods may have been unorthodox and even illegal, but as a child, I learned how to survive, create, and build. I knew I loved Shay, but could I achieve that deep, abiding loving relationship I so desperately wanted? The type of love that was inconsistent between my parents. I knew I had work to do, I heard a voice from deep within telling me I needed help.

I often reflected on you can't be what you can't see. How was I going to emulate the love she needed, when I didn't have an example? This was foreign territory for me. I thought to myself, who would help me? Can someone help me? I knew I needed hope to overcome these obstacles, and without opportunities, I would lose hope. I had lived a life of adverse childhood experiences including homelessness, food insecurities, and the complete lack of parental support or guidance.

For years it was about survival. I was able to shift my mind to motivation mode to keep myself alive when I had nothing to eat and when I was living in that abandoned house without running water or heat. Even in my darkest, coldest days, I somehow believed life could be different.

With all I had overcome, I held on to the belief I could convince Shay that we could build a life together. I knew I loved her, and I wanted the love that I felt from her. But there were just too many issues in my life for her to deal with. She left me on May 7, 2022. Watching her leave was difficult, I felt alone, really alone. Why hadn't I felt this way before when others walked out of my life?

Shay had her struggles too, especially dealing with the fact that she was adopted. She decided to seek therapy to help her with the clashing feelings she was dealing with. Shay also decided to take a chance and suggest that I might benefit from counseling. I was conflicted about the thought of this, therapy was frowned upon amongst Black men from the hood. Black men from the streets don't need anyone telling them how to act or feel. Seeing a therapist was a sign of weakness. We were considered deficient in some way if we had to seek counseling. Regardless, Shay gave me the number of her therapist, making the call was on me. I looked at the number several times and contemplated if I should make the call.

I knew God used people, things, and signs to speak to us. I thought that, perhaps, Shay was God's vehicle leading me to counseling. Seeing her walk out of my life had been gut-wrenching. Putting my ego, and pride aside, I made the call that same day. I told Shay and my children that I was going into therapy. My son Rowdy was supportive saying he was proud of me.

On June 9, 2022, I had my first appointment with a therapist. I went in with an open mind thinking, let's see what he has to offer. It couldn't hurt to listen. When I walked into the office, I was face-to-face with a short White man, with thick gray hair, and brown-rimmed glasses in his mid-to-late 60s.

The soft-spoken man greeted me and offered me a seat. I stated, *"Doc, I don't know where to start."* Dr. Gerace looked squarely at me, *"Well, tell me why you are here."* Shay leaving me came tumbling out. Her leaving me brought a level of sadness that was unequal to anything I had experienced. The emotional wall I lived behind would not permit any tears or another outward show of sadness.

Dr. Gerace asked me why I felt so sad that Shay had left me. I told him that I loved her more than any other woman I had been with. In the past, if a woman left, I just moved on to someone else. Dr. Gerace explained that this feeling represented who I truly am as a person. I was taken aback by this statement. I wondered how I could be a person with such deep feelings. I had never even thought about how I felt about anything.

I shared that I could come off as a little controlling sometimes. I am uptight in my surroundings, telling Dr. Gerace that I don't like when people come to my house unannounced. I am always on guard at the house. I didn't want to be prey for anyone. I always had to be strong, and could not reveal any weaknesses, sadness, or uncertainties. I also admitted being selfish especially when it came to food. Further elaborating on my food issues saying that when I was 12 and living in an abandoned house with my Uncle BL, he would often eat the little bit of food I had when I fell asleep.

Dr. Gerace told me I wasn't that 12-year-old starving boy anymore. He also told me that I had post-traumatic stress syndrome and it's why I am always so guarded and always felt like I was under attack. These were all revelations to me. As a result, there was never a time after that first meeting that I didn't know what to discuss during my sessions. I had felt an instant connection with Dr. Gerace. I trusted him. Nothing was off the table for discussion. Opening up to him in many ways was a relief I didn't know I needed.

The traumas I experienced during my early life forced me to create a persona that would keep me safe. I felt that being a wolf was what kept me alive. I was always ready to attack and felt a desperate need to survive, be the hunter vs. the hunted, staying safe from bullets and abuse. Throughout my life, I thought that the wolf
persona was the real me. Thinking back, I expressed that the wolf persona was initially created after the sexual abuse I

had experienced at the hands of my cousin Lil' Tony when I was seven. I suppressed memories of what happened. It was like wearing a mask. My father would call me gay if I showed any emotion about anything, so all emotions were denied.

One of the hardest things about revealing the sexual abuse is whether you will be believed. If it happens while you're younger, you try to understand how someone could do this to you. You're then conflicted about whether it is your fault or not. Then you try to put it out of your mind as if it were all just a bad dream. I've learned that as much as you want it to go away, it won't if you never talk about it. At times it finds ways to manifest the hurt you experienced through your actions, unknowingly I might add. I have no problem sharing my sexual trauma with others now. Hopefully, it helps someone and gives them the confidence to speak out about it.

Slowly, over the weeks and months in therapy, I learned what may have been apparent to only a select few, my life was total trauma. I tried to resist this revelation, but it was true. As Dr. Gerace guided me through the sessions, he told me the trauma did not have
to define who I was. I learned that I had a choice. For the first time, I began to see myself differently. The Bible says that a man without a plan and a vision will fail. Because of therapy and my strong belief in God, my plan and vision were being redefined. I had been letting what happened to me control

me all of these years. Knowing I had a choice in how it affects me has been so freeing. I have become very intentional about everything I am doing and strengthening my walk with God.

I had never believed I would live to be 15-years old or 18 or even 21. To still be alive at 48, and noticing the small joys in life is like a miracle to me. I find contentment in just watching the wind blow the tree branches, breathing in fresh air, and enjoying the sounds of laughter. There was a seismic shift in my life. I felt a different kind of strength than I always had. I was done being the wolf and changing guns to carry as often as I changed my clothes.

While the rebirth had begun, a new trauma confronted me. It was Sunday, June 5, 2022, I clearly remember the phone call at 3:16 a.m. that morning from my God-sister, Jodi. She told me, *"Your mom has been found unresponsive."* I thought was dreaming, but she said it again, *"Ra they found your mom unresponsive."* This can't be, she didn't have any known illnesses. I had
spoken to my mom the night before at 10:50 pm. She told me she was about to go to bed, so she could be ready when I picked her up in the morning to go to church with me. She had been attending church with me regularly since Shay left. I had just revealed to her on Thursday leading up to this call that I finally love her again like the way I did when I was eight.

I was awakened by this horrible news. This can't be happening again. My heart sank. I rushed to Temple Hospital where my mom had been taken. Once there, I was able to assess the severity of her condition. My mom had been without oxygen for an extended period and doctors told me that she was near death. I didn't want to accept that. God wouldn't let this happen I thought to myself. I just got to a place of loving my mom in a way that I thought I never would again.

The pain in my heart stung as if it was pierced with a burning knife. After reconciling to this degree, I believed I would have many wonderful days ahead to spend with my mom and now she could be taken away from me. Jodi and I visited my mother daily for just over two weeks. I placed restrictions on her receiving any other visitors because the doctor told me that she would need lots of rest if she were to have a chance to recover. Too many visitors would overstimulate her brain, and reduce the chances of her recovering.

Then it happened, on Thursday, June 23, 2022, I received the dreaded phone call from the doctor that my mom had passed. A calmness settled over me as I had been preparing for the inevitable. God gave me peace in this tragedy. Finally, the demons she battled in her life associated with drug addiction were over and she would not have to battle anymore.

She had been clean for a little over five years; however, she revealed to me on May 29, 2022, that the devil had woke her up in the middle of the night and tempted her to buy a bag of blow. She said, *"Son, I knew that was the enemy because the urge was so intense, and I haven't snorted in five years."* Needless to say, she didn't resist for too long. I learned that she gave in to the temptation that Saturday once she got off the phone with me.

Unbeknownst to her, the coke she was used to buying was now being cut with Fentanyl, and immediately after her first snort, she went into cardiac arrest. I knew she was at peace now, spending eternity with the Lord. My brothers looked to me for strength as they grappled with her passing. As I had always done, I took charge and made all of my mom's final arrangements.

For the first time in my life, I could genuinely express my emotions. I could show my feelings. As a wolf, nothing had fazed me. But as part of the process of my rebirth, my emotions were on display. I cried at her funeral. For a second, I felt alone, but remembered that God was always with me. I got to mourn her death properly, no hang-ups, no fear of what people thought, just a man mourning the loss of his mom. It was a summer of intense reflection and growth for me, I completed my master's degree while reconciling all of my emotions surrounding her loss.

On October 15, 2022, God took me from what I was as a man and made me confront my issues and share them. As difficult as it was, my communication with Shay became very transparent. I thought I was going to take what happened with Lil' Tony to my grave. For Shay, hearing about the abuse gave her a different perspective of me. She told me that she knew I was very special and that God would help me get through.

I credit my devotion to Christ and Dr. Gerace as keys to my rebirth. It was my foundation with God that ultimately made me confront the traumatic issues in my life. God had to tear me down before he could build me back up. I didn't know where to turn, I had felt completely helpless. Shay leaving was the triggering
event that unknowingly started me on this new path, my rebirth. I knew I needed to do something different, to be my true self.

Dr. Gerace had told me that I needed to learn about who my true self was. I turned to God for help. Through continual prayers, reflection, and counseling, new pathways of myself began to emerge.

After working for months on how to communicate with my heart, Shay and I were married on June 3, 2023. We became a brood of seven with my three children, Arti, Rowdy, and Nya, and Shay's children, Darius, Cheyenne, and Emmi. Little Savanna, 5, the child we share, sparkled inside and out as my newly blended family of nine celebrated our union. It was something I thought only happened on television, but it was happening. All that I ever hoped for was finally a reality.

My maternal grandfather, Ray Ballenger, used to tell me that, *"If you don't stand for something, you will fall for anything. As long as you are standing for what is right."* I had chosen to stand for Jesus, so I was not going to fail.

At my wedding, I was chatting with my old friend Tariq, who had been with me during my early hustling days. We talked about the stigma of seeking help from a therapist. Riq had told me that some memories had begun eating away at him of late. So, he understood it when I told him that perhaps therapy would help.

Months later Riq told me that he too was still struggling with past memories and it might be time for him to go into therapy. He said he too, learned, that what we experienced as kids and teens wasn't normal. It was traumatic. We agreed that seeing a therapist and showing any emotions was frowned upon because it would make us appear soft. Now we both know and can clearly articulate the misinformation we had been fed as children.

Confronting trauma and seeking help to unravel the complexities of my life, and hearing similar words from Riq, I often told to the mostly minority students at the school where I was the principal, *"I understand you can't be what you can't see. Some of you would not think you could be a principal until you saw me."* I dressed like them. I breathed like them and I spoke frankly to them. I am just like a regular guy from the hood they *can* identify with. They recognize that they *could* be me.

All those years ago, my principal, Mr. Romanelli, that heavy-set, bald white man, though kind, was not someone I could identify with. Even though Mr. Romanelli knew how intelligent I was, there was no reciprocal connection. It was sheer determination, and my desperate need for survival, that propelled me to strive for and actively participate in my education. I achieved what no one, except perhaps the GED teacher in prison, thought was possible for a kid who had dropped out of the 10th grade.

As a child, teen, and into adulthood, my day-to-day life was far different from anything most people would experience. Through it all, I never lost hope for a better life, which for me had come from watching television shows about families. I had no positive role models in my life that I could identify with. Yet I know how critically important they are. A friend recently texted me thanking me for being someone who gives strength to others to face day-to-day problems. He told me that no one knocks him down because truth sustains him. He was thankful to God for giving him a genuine brother like me.

Going through some of the worst times in life, you can encounter one person, maybe two, who plant seeds of hope in your life. For me, those seeds were planted years apart, from some of the unlikeliest people, and in some instances, chance encounters.

One seed came from my elementary school principal, Mr. Romanelli, a bald, heavy-set, White man, who believed in me enough to tell me that I was smart, and encouraged me to stay out of trouble. Another seed came from a fairly young, nice-looking, black woman who prepared me to take and pass my GED in jail. After learning that I had passed the test with an excellent score, she told me that I was smart and that I could go to college. The last seed to be planted in my life came from a man who had been on death row for 27 years that I befriended while playing chess. He told me that if I have ten negative friends, I am bound to be the eleventh. This seed was much different from the two other seeds planted in my life, but it was relevant because of my socialization from being on the streets.

Had I not been truly listening to their conversations, those comments, those seeds of hope, I might have missed them. Two seeds planted by two different individuals over twenty years apart were about me being smart. It clicked for me when I was released from the cartel and given my life back. I remembered what Mr. Romanelli and my GED teacher said, which gave me the confidence and encouragement I needed to know that I could succeed in life. The last seed planted by the former death row inmate unlocked the mental barriers placed in my mind due to my socialization.

Growing up I would usually hear people in the hood talk negatively about other Black folks who decided to move out of the hood and establish a new friend group. People would say those people think that they are better than the people still in the hood, and they forgot where they came from. This kind of thinking kept me trapped, along with countless other people. We didn't want to appear like those people; therefore, we had a blind loyalty to an environment and way of thinking that would ultimately lead to our demise if nothing changed.

I now know that I can never forget where I come from because it has influenced part of who I am. My willingness to accept that the other parts of me were just as valid was influenced by those seeds that were planted.

I am gratified to know that I can be a role model for others. I believe it is important to deliver a message of hope to those impacted by trauma and adverse childhood experiences. I deliver a message of hope in three words: See Me. *Now*.

Acknowledgments

All praise and glory to **my Lord and Savior Jesus Christ**. You are my rock, my redeemer, my restorer. Everything that I am, everything that I have, and everything this book represents is because of You. This is not just my story—it is Your story through me.

To **Grandmom Lula** (*Grem*) **Williams**, you planted the seed of Christ in my heart. That seed took root, grew strong, and continues to bear fruit in every area of my life.

To **my mother and father, Yolanda and Michael Williams**—thank you for your love, sacrifice, and strength. You laid the foundation for everything I've become. I'm standing tall today because of you.

To **my wife, Sharon Hamilton**—you are my heartbeat, my partner, and my peace. Your love fills in every space that once felt empty. You believed in this book when it was still just an idea, and you believed in me before I knew what I was capable of. You are my sun on a cloudy day, the missing piece of the puzzle to my life.

To **my children—Arti, Rowdy, Peaches, Dar, Cheytown, EM&M, and Turkey Meatloaf**—you are each a living part of my journey, and I love you deeply. Your lives inspire me. Your love strengthens me. Your presence gives me purpose.

To **my brothers, Erc and Meat**—

Erc, thank you for always supporting me. You've always been consistent, present, and proud.
Meat, we lived through things together that only we fully understand, especially one particular moment. To the readers: you'll have to read the story to understand that part.

To **Sean Turner** (Shizz)—your fellowship, spiritual guidance, and realness helped keep me aligned in truth and humility. Thank you for being a brother in faith and life.

To **Marquita Clement** *(Mom Kita)*—you hold me spiritually accountable, and I'm grateful for it. Thank you for your consistent love, encouragement, and feedback throughout this project.

To **Sean Cave**—thank you for capturing the photo at Chestnut Hill College that ended up on the cover of this book. That image says more than words could ever express.

To **John**—an unlikely teacher in an unlikely place. Jail isn't where most expect to meet wisdom, but you taught me some of the most valuable life lessons in that season. I haven't forgotten them.

To **Dale Hollenbach**—thank you for reading through nearly every chapter alongside Dr. Joyce Jeuell as we worked through the heart and rhythm of this story. Your insight and encouragement were invaluable.

To **Lawrence and Taneka Davis** *(LJ and T)*—my extended family. You didn't just read drafts—you poured into them with love and gave thoughtful, honest feedback. Thank you for standing with me in this journey.

To **Bob Stewart** and **Gillian Gutteridge**—you both read the early chapters and pushed us with feedback that helped elevate this book. You helped us step into a higher level of storytelling, and we thank you for that.

To **Dr. Jeanne Dagna**, your role as a sensitivity reader brought deep insight, helping us honor the reader's emotional journey without compromising the authenticity or integrity of the message. Thank you for helping us make this book as thoughtful as it is truthful.

To **Susanne Harkins**—thank you for arranging the use of the Rotunda at Chestnut Hill College, a space that added dignity and presence to this journey. Your effort behind the scenes did not go unnoticed.

To **Donna Dello Buono**, thank you for your critical role in the editing process. Your skill, patience, and dedication helped shape the finality of this project.

To **Chestnut Hill College**—thank you for being the place where I earned my **Criminal Justice** and **Educational Leadership** degrees, and where I met some of the most influential people in my journey. Thank you for being a place of growth, learning, and self-discovery. You provided the academic foundation, but more importantly, a space where I found my voice.

To **Dr. Joyce Jeuell**, my co-author, thank you for recognizing the power in my story, which began with a simple classroom introduction. You saw potential in me

and in this work long before it was on paper. You helped me bring it to life with courage, compassion, and commitment. Your partnership means everything.

To the **students, families, and communities** we've had the honor to serve, your resilience, honesty, and humanity breathe life into every page of this book. Thank you for letting us walk beside you.

To our **mentors, friends, and colleagues**—thank you for sharpening us, challenging us, and standing with us through the process.

And finally, to **you**, the reader, thank you for joining us on this journey. May this book inspire you to own your truth, walk in your purpose, and never doubt the power of redemption.

With humility, strength, and everlasting faith,
Rafiq Williams, Dr. Joyce Vottima Jeuell, and Anne Fahy Morris

Meet the Authors

Rafiq Williams is a Christian, father, motivator, and educator. He currently serves as Dean of Students at a public high school in Delaware. He worked at an approved private school for students with special education needs and various diagnoses for over a decade. He began as a teaching assistant at that school and worked his way to leading the school as the principal. He overcame teenage homelessness, and incarceration on the way to earning his Master of Education from Chestnut Hill College. He also

holds a principal certification for grades K12. He is married to Sharon Hamilton and is the father of a blended family of seven. He is the proud grandfather of six grandchildren. He lives in Delaware.

Joyce Vottima Jeuell has spent her career in education as a teacher, an administrator, and a college professor. She also wrote about education for the Philadelphia Inquirer. Dr. Jeuell worked in public schools as a secondary special education teacher before becoming a high school assistant principal and a middle school principal. She taught college classes in education at Immaculata University and as an

Assistant Professor of Education and supervisor of the Principal's Leadership Program at Chestnut Hill College. She is the proud mother of two sons, two bonus "daughters," and Glam Mom of three adorable grandchildren living in suburban Philadelphia.

Anne Fahy Morris is a journalist and educator. She covered national news for the Associated Press and wrote  for The Trentonian and The Philadelphia Inquirer. She received a Master of Science in education from the University of Pennsylvania and combines both disciplines in her writing today. She is a mother of four and lives outside Philadelphia.

www.ingramcontent.com/pod-product-compliance
Lightning Source LLC
Chambersburg PA
CBHW060348190426
43201CB00043B/1766